THE ESSENCE OF
Self-Realization

The disciple with his guru

THE ESSENCE OF
Self-Realization

THE WISDOM OF PARAMHANSA YOGANANDA

Recorded, compiled and edited by
Swami Kriyananda

"The truth simply is.
It cannot be voted into existence.
It must be perceived by every individual
in the changeless Self within."
—Paramhansa Yogananda

crystal clarity publishers
nevada city, california

Crystal Clarity Publishers, Nevada City, CA 95959
© Copyright 2009, 1990 by Hansa Trust
All rights reserved. Published 2012
First edition 1990. Second edition 2009

ISBN: 978-1-56589-239-2
First edition ISBN: 0-916124-29-0
Printed in the China

Cover design by Renée Glenn Designs
Interior design by Crystal Clarity Publishers

Library of Congress Cataloging-in-Publication Data
Yogananda, Paramhansa, 1893-1952.
   The Essence of Self-Realization : the Wisdom of Paramhansa
Yogananda / recorded and compiled by Swami Kriyananda. — 2nd
ed.
      p. cm.
   Includes index.
   ISBN 978-1-56589-239-2 (trade paper, indexed)
   1. Spiritual life. I. Kriyananda, Swami. II. Title.

   BP605.S43Y64 2008
   294.5'44—dc22
                                        2008040416

800-424-1055
www.crystalclarity.com

DEDICATED

With love and humility
to all his disciples

CONTENTS

INTRODUCTION

I lived with Paramhansa Yogananda as a disciple for the last three and a half years of his life. After I'd been with him a year and a half, he began urging me to write down things that he was saying during informal conversations. We were at his desert retreat, where he was completing his commentaries on the Bhagavad Gita.

At first, I found myself in some difficulty. I knew no shorthand, and my handwriting was daunting to read, even for me. The Master, however, true to his own teaching that one should concentrate on light instead of on darkness, paid no attention to such insignificant handicaps. He kept on urging me.

"I don't often speak from a level of *gyana* [impersonal wisdom]," he said. His nature usually found expression in divine love.

My enthusiasm grew as I realized that nowhere else had I ever read or heard teachings so profound, so clear, and so convincing.

"Write that down!" he would call out to me over the years that followed, during conversations with the monks or with visitors. Sometimes, in explanation, he would add, "I've never said that before."

My penmanship being what it was, I could never hope to keep up with him. As weeks passed, however, I discovered that he had bestowed on me an extraordinary blessing. I was able to hear his voice afterward, as if speaking the words in my mind as I wrote them down. So remarkable was his blessing that, years later in India, I was able to verify my memory of words, and even of whole sentences, that he'd uttered in Hindi or Bengali, both of which languages were unknown to me when he was alive.

Even today, the memory of his words and of his voice rings clearly in my mind, rich with wisdom, divine love, and the fullness of spiritual power—frequently combined with a delightful sense of humor. His conversations were sprinkled with anecdotes; they sparkled with metaphors, and contained the deepest insight into all levels of reality, human and divine, that I have ever had the great blessing to encounter.

Swami Kriyananda
Ananda World Brotherhood Village
Nevada City, California

Editorial Note

*P*aramhansa means, "supreme swan." The highest spiritual title in the Hindu religion, its origins are rooted in ancient lore.

The swan is at home equally on dry land and on water. The true sage, or *paramhansa*, similarly, is at home equally in the realms of matter and of the Spirit.

The swan also, according to Indian tradition, is able to separate milk from water. Perhaps what this means, literally, is that the swan secretes a substance in its beak that curdles milk, thereby separating the curds from the whey. Whatever the biological facts, in India the swan symbolizes the ability of a Self-realized master to separate the solid substance of truth from the insubstantiality of delusion.

Hansa, finally and most importantly, is a composite of two Sanskrit words meaning, "I am He," or, "I am Spirit." Thus, a *paramhansa* is one who is in a position to proclaim his oneness with Spirit—supremely so, for he no longer merely affirms it mentally, but has realized its truth in his inner Self.

According to Sanskrit scholars, "paramhansa" is more properly written, *paramahansa*, with an extra *a* in the middle. Scholarly precision, however, doesn't always coincide with unscholarly comprehension.

In English, that middle *a* increases the problem of pronunciation to the point where people pause there, and thus give emphasis to a letter that, in India, is unpronounced. The average American or Englishman, in other words, and very likely the average non-Indian, pronounces the word thus:

"param*aa*hansa." The correct pronunciation, however, is *paramhansa.*

For Westerners who want simply to know, with some degree of accuracy, how to pronounce this, to us, difficult word, Sanskrit scholars accept the spelling, paramhansa.

Chapter 1

THE FOLLY OF MATERIALISM

— 1 —

"The truth simply *is*. It cannot be voted into existence. It must be perceived by every individual in the changeless Self within."

— 2 —

Paramhansa Yogananda said: "The material scientist uses the forces of nature to make the environment of man better and more comfortable. The spiritual scientist uses mind-power to enlighten the soul.

"Mind-power shows man the way to inner happiness, which gives him immunity to outer inconveniences.

"Of the two types of scientist, which would you say renders the greater service? The spiritual scientist, surely."

— 3 —

"What is the use of spending all one's time on things that don't last? The drama of life has for its moral the fact that it is merely that: a drama, an illusion.

"Fools, imagining the play to be real and lasting, weep through the sad parts, grieve that the happy parts cannot endure, and sorrow that the play must, at last, come to an end. Suffering is the punishment for their spiritual blindness.

"The wise, however, seeing the drama for the utter delusion it is, seek eternal happiness in the Self within.

"Life, for those who don't know how to handle it, is a terrible machine. Sooner or later it cuts them to pieces."

--⊷4⊷--

A man whom Paramhansa Yogananda met in New York complained to him, "I can never forgive myself for taking thirty-five years to make my first million dollars!"

"You still are not satisfied?" inquired the Master.

"Far from it!" lamented the businessman. "A friend of mine has made several times that. Now I won't be happy until I've made forty million!"

Paramhansa Yogananda, recalling this episode years later, ended his account of it by saying, "Before that man could make his forty million and settle down to spending the rest of his days in peace and happiness, he suffered a complete nervous breakdown. Soon afterwards, he died.

"Such is the fruit of excessive worldly ambition."

--⊷5⊷--

Yogananda said: "I once saw a cartoon drawing of a dog hitched to a small, but well-laden, cart. The dog's owner had found an ingenious method for getting it to pull the cart for him. A long pole, tied to the cart, extended forward over the dog's head. At the end of the pole there dangled a sausage, temptingly. The dog, straining in vain to reach that sausage, hardly noticed the heavy cart he was dragging along behind him.

"How many business people are like that! They keep thinking, 'If I can make just a little more money, I'll find happiness at last.' Somehow, their 'sausage of happiness' keeps receding from their grasp. As they strain to reach it, however, just see what a cart-load of troubles and worries they drag along behind them!"

6

"Possession of material riches, without inner peace, is like dying of thirst while bathing in a lake. If material poverty is to be avoided, spiritual poverty is to be abhorred! It is spiritual poverty, not material lack, that lies at the core of all human suffering."

7

"People forget that the price of luxury is an ever-increasing expenditure of nerve and brain energy, and the consequent shortening of their natural life span.

"Materialists become so engrossed in the task of making money that they can't relax enough to enjoy their comforts even after they've acquired them.

"How unsatisfactory is modern life! Just look at the people around you. Ask yourself, are they happy? See the sad expressions on so many faces. Observe the emptiness in their eyes.

"A materialistic life tempts mankind with smiles and assurances, but is consistent only in this: It never fails, eventually, to break all its promises!"

8

"Behind every rosebush of pleasure there lies hidden a rattlesnake of suffering and pain."

→✱ 9 ✱←

Addressing a large audience in America, Paramhansa Yogananda said, "Modern man takes pride in his scientific approach to reality. Let me then make this proposal: that you analyze life itself—in a laboratory, as it were. Americans love to experiment, so why not experiment on yourselves: on your attitudes toward life, on your thoughts and behavior?

"Find out what life is, and how human life might be improved. Discover what people most deeply want in life, and what is the best way for them to achieve that hearts' desire. Find what it is they most want to avoid, and how they might, in future, avoid this unwelcome 'guest.'

"In physics and chemistry, if a person wants the right answers he must ask the right questions. The same is true also in life. Try to find out why so many people are unhappy. Then, having understood that, seek the best way of achieving lasting happiness.

"Insist on finding practical solutions—formulas that will work for everyone. One's approach to life should be as scientific as the physicist's, to his study of the universe.

"Religion itself should adopt a more scientific approach to life. It should seek practical solutions to life's fundamental problems.

"Indeed, spiritual principles offer the most universally practical solutions there are."

⊸ 10 ⊸

"A baby cries for a toy only until he gets it. Then he throws it away and cries for something else.

"Isn't that the way of the worldly man in his ceaseless pursuit of happiness? As soon as he gets one thing, he loses interest in it and goes rushing in pursuit of something else. Nothing in this world ever satisfies him for long."

⊸ 11 ⊸

"The soul cannot find its lost happiness in material things for the simple reason that the comfort they offer is counterfeit. Having lost contact with divine bliss within, man hopes to satisfy his need for it in the pseudo-pleasures of the senses. On deeper levels of his being, however, he remains aware of his former, supernal state in God. True satisfaction eludes him, for what he seeks, while rushing restlessly from one sense pleasure to another, is his lost happiness in the Lord.

"Ah, blindness! How long must you continue before, suffering from satiety, boredom, and disgust, you seek joy within, where alone it can be found?"

Chapter 2

THE TRUE PURPOSE OF LIFE

1

"Those who are immersed in body-consciousness are like strangers in a foreign land. Our native country is Omnipresence. On earth we are but travelers—guests on a brief visit.

"Unfortunately, most people make undesirable guests of themselves! They insist on monopolizing a small portion of this earth as their very own. Their constant thought is, 'my home, my wife, my husband, my children.' Material entanglements, sweet and mysterious, keep them dreaming through the sleep of delusion. They forget who and what they really are.

"Wake up! before your dream of life vanishes into the infinite. When this body drops in death, where will your family be? your home? your money? You are not this body. The body is only a plate, given to you that you might eat from it the feast of Spirit.

"Why not learn this essential lesson before death? Why wait? Don't tie yourself to the limitations of human consciousness, but remember the vastness of the Spirit within."

2

"'Get away,' Krishna said, 'from My ocean of suffering and misery!' With God, life is a feast of happiness, but without Him it is a nest of troubles, pains, and disappointments."

⊸⤙⊸ 3 ⊸⤚⊸

"The purpose of human life is not marriage and eating and death. To eat and drink and die is the way of the animals. Why live below your true station in life?

"God gave you intelligence that you might use it properly, to solve the mystery of your existence. He made you intelligent that you might develop the discrimination to seek Him. Use this divine gift wisely. Not to do so is to do yourself the greatest possible injustice."

⊸⤙⊸ 4 ⊸⤚⊸

"The true purpose of life is to know God. Worldly temptations were given you to help you develop discrimination: Will you prefer sense pleasures, or will you choose God? Pleasures seem alluring at first, but if you choose them, sooner or later you will find yourself enmeshed in endless troubles and difficulties.

"Loss of health, of peace of mind, and of happiness is the lot of everyone who succumbs to the lure of sense pleasures. Infinite joy, on the other hand, is yours once you know God.

"Every human being will have, eventually, to learn this great lesson of life."

—◦ 5 ◦—

"See the lights of a city twinkling at a distance. Don't they look beautiful? Yet some of those very lights may be illuminating great crimes.

"Don't be deceived by life's outward show. Its glamour is superficial. Look behind appearances, to the eternal truth within."

—◦ 6 ◦—

"You were not born merely to make money, have children, and then die! Yours is a glorious destiny. You are a child of the Infinite! Every fulfillment you ever dreamed of lies waiting for you in God. His infinite treasure-house is yours. Why delay? Why waste time on countless detours? Go straight to Him."

—◦ 7 ◦—

"Think for a moment what Jesus meant when he said, 'Let the dead bury their dead.'[1] His meaning was that most people are dead but don't know it! They have no ambition, no initiative, no spiritual enthusiasm, no joy in life.

"What is the use of living that way? Life should be a constant inspiration. To live mechanically is to be dead inside though your body be still breathing!

"The reason people's lives are so dull and uninteresting is that they depend on shallow channels for their happiness, instead of going to the limitless source of all joy within themselves."

"This universe is a dream of God's. Its very vastness suggests the limitlessness of consciousness.

"Just imagine a sphere of light. Visualize it expanding through eternity with the speed of thought. Could it ever reach a point where further expansion was impossible? Never! Though matter has limitations, consciousness has none.

"Don't you see? That is what this universe is: infinite, because the capacities of consciousness are infinite. Even as thought precedes action, so matter, like that expanding sphere of light, filled the space which thought had created for it.

"The basic substance of the universe is consciousness. Matter itself was simply thought into existence—first as energy, and then as matter. For matter is only energy on a grosser level of manifestation. Modern science has made this discovery.

"And scientific meditation long ago made the discovery that cosmic energy is simply a projection of the will of God."

⊷⊶ 9 ⊷⊶

"Man is not important for his ego and personality. He is important because, as a soul, he is a part of God."

⟶ 10 ⟵

"These few years of your earth life are just so many seconds compared to the eons before you were born, and to the endless reaches of time still to come, long after you leave this world. Why be identified with this brief material interlude? These are not *your* body, *your* family, *your* country. You are only a visitor here. Your homeland is Infinity. Your true life-span is eternity."

⟶ 11 ⟵

"People live too much vicariously, in the opinions of others. If you want to 'have life, and have it more abundantly,'[2] as Jesus taught, you must begin by living your own life, not that of anyone else! Your primary concern should be how to win the Lord, not how to please your fellowman.

"Never lose sight of God. This world will go on without you. You are not as important as you think! Into the dustbin of ages countless billions of people have been thrown. It is the Lord's recognition we must cultivate, not other people's."

⟶ 12 ⟵

"The purpose of human life is to find God. That is the only reason for our existence. Job, friends, material interests—these things in themselves mean nothing. They can never provide you with true happiness, for the simple reason that none of them, in itself, is complete. Only God encompasses everything.

"That is why Jesus said, 'Seek ye first the kingdom of God, and all these things shall be added unto you.'[3] Seek ye first the Giver of all gifts, and you shall receive from Him all His gifts of lesser fulfillment."

1   Matthew 8:22.
2   John 10:10.
3   Matthew 6:33

Chapter 3

THE DREAM NATURE OF THE UNIVERSE

⟶➤ 1 ➤⟵

"There was a farmer standing by a tree, absorbed in thought. His wife came rushing up, weeping, to announce that their only son had just been killed by a cobra. The farmer made no reply. Stunned by his seeming indifference, the wife cried, 'You are heartless!'

"'You don't understand,' the farmer replied. 'Last night I dreamed that I was a king, and that I had seven sons. They went out into the forest and all were bitten by cobras and died. Now I am wondering whether I ought to weep for my seven dead sons in that dream, or for our one son who has just been killed in this dream we are dreaming now.'

"The farmer was a man of spiritual vision. To him, the material world and the subconscious dream-world were both equally unreal.

"When we dream at night, this present dream fades into unreality, and only that subconscious dream-world seems real to us. When we return again to the dream of this world, that other dream is forgotten.

"Everything exists only in consciousness."

⟶➤ 2 ➤⟵

"A man is sleeping, and dreams that he is a soldier. He goes into battle, fights bravely, then is fatally wounded. Sadly he dreams of his approaching death, perhaps thinking of the dear ones he must leave behind.

"Suddenly he wakes up. In joyful relief he cries, 'Ah! I am not a soldier, and I am not dying! It was only a dream.' And he laughs to find himself alive and well.

"But what of the soldier who actually fights in this earth-life, and is wounded and killed? Suddenly, in the astral world, he wakes up to find that it was all just a dream; that in that other world he has no physical body, no flesh to be wounded, no bones to be broken.

"Don't you see? All the experiences of this world are like that. They are nothing but dream experiences."

-⟫ 3 ⟪-

"Time and space form the imaginary framework on which was constructed the vast universe.

"Suppose I am asleep, and I dream that I board an airplane in Los Angeles and travel 12,000 miles to India. On awaking, I see that that whole experience occurred in the little space of my own brain, and that the actual time elapsed was, perhaps, just a few seconds.

"Such is the delusion of time and space, on which we base all our human conceptions of reality."

-⟫ 4 ⟪-

"This world seems real to you because God dreamed *you* into existence along with His cosmic dream. You are a part of His dream.

"If, at night, you dream that you bump your head against a wall, you may get an imaginary pain in your head. The moment you awake, however, you realize that there was no wall there to hurt you. The pain you experienced was in your mind, but not in your head!

"The same is true of this dream you are dreaming now. Wake up to the one Reality, God, and you will see that this earth life is just a show. It is nothing but shadows and light!"

∽ 5 ∾

"In a movie, the action seems very real. If you look up to the projection booth, however, you will see that that whole story is being produced by a single beam of light.

"That is how it is in this great 'movie' of creation. 'God said, Let there be light.'[1] Out of the great beam of cosmic light was manifested the entire universe. It is a cosmic movie, in many ways like the one in the movie theater.

"Much of the difference is in degree. In the movie theater, what you behold is two-dimensional, and is true only to the senses of sight and sound. The cosmic movie is three-dimensional, and is true also to the senses of taste, smell, and touch.

"The movie you see in the movie theater may move you to laughter and tears. How much more compelling, then, is God's movie, involving as it does the sense of depth, and not two senses only, but five!

"This life, however, is no more real than a movie."

∽ 6 ∾

"It is a pleasant fancy," commented a physicist condescendingly, "to think of trees, flowers, and rivers as God's dream. Science, however, has revealed that all things, in essence, are the same. They are merely masses of protons and electrons."

The Master was quick to respond to this challenge. "If you dumped a load of bricks on the ground," he said, "would they form themselves into a house? Hardly! It takes intelligence to make something meaningful of a heap of bricks.

"Protons and electrons are the building-bricks of creation. It took great intelligence to shape them into all the forms we behold in Nature: flowers and trees, mountains, streams, and thinking human beings."

--⬤ 7 ⬤--

"Where did the material come from to create the universe? Before creation, there was only God.

"It would be no explanation at all to say, 'The Lord is omnipotent; He can perform any miracle.' Even miracles must have some basis in reality.

"God is conscious, or else He isn't God. In whatever way He produced matter, then, it had to come about as an act of His consciousness. The universe cannot be real except as a manifestation of that consciousness.

"If this is true, and it cannot but be true, then consciousness is the reality, and matter, the illusion.

"Science itself endorses this statement, at least to the extent of showing that matter *as we know it* is an illusion. What we see around us are not solid rocks, towering trees, flowing rivers, and corporeal beings, each one different from all others. Behind those appearances are whirling masses of atoms. Even the atoms are an illusion, for behind them lies an ocean of energy manifesting itself through the atoms as rocks, trees, water, and human and animal bodies.

"Behind cosmic energy, finally, are the thoughts of God.

"This isn't to say that the physical universe is not real. Its reality, however, is not what it appears to be. The underlying reality of everything is consciousness.

"God dreamed the universe into existence."

-»8»-

"Who made God?" a visitor asked. The Master smiled.

"Many ask that question. Because they live in the realm of causation, they imagine that nothing can exist without a cause. God, however, the Supreme Cause, is beyond causation. It is not necessary that He, in turn, have a creator.

"How could the Absolute depend for Its existence on another Absolute?"

-»9»-

"It is a mistake, really, to say that God created the universe. He didn't create it—at least not in the way a carpenter would construct a table.

"God *became* the universe. Without in any way altering His intrinsic nature, He manifested a portion of His consciousness as *maya*, the cosmic illusion.

"Nothing is as it appears to be. All that exists is a manifestation of the thoughts of God."

-»10»-

"How did God, the one Reality, manifest this universe of appearances? He did so through the law of duality.

"His one consciousness took on the appearance of opposites: of positive and negative, of light and darkness, of pleasure and pain, and so on to an infinity of contrasting illusions.

"A part of His consciousness moved. As the Bible tells us, 'And the Spirit of God moved upon the face of the waters.'[2] We might compare that motion to the motion of waves on the surface of the ocean. The ocean level never changes even when the waves rise very high, for every upward movement at one place is compensated for by a downward movement at another. The over-all water level remains ever the same.

"Even so, God, the Ocean of Spirit, remains unaltered by His creation. At the 'surface' of His consciousness, however, His spirit moves, and that movement, or vibration, produces duality, like the rising and falling of the waves on the sea.

"The Infinite One vibrated a part of Himself to become two, then many, until the Cosmic Vibration produced stars and galaxies and planets, flowers and trees and human bodies.

"The Cosmic Vibration is called *Aum.* It is the *Amen* in the Book of Revelation in the Bible. It is the *Word* in the Gospel of St. John. It is the 'music of the spheres' of the ancient Greeks. It is the *Amin* of the Muslims, the *Ahunavar* of the Zoroastrians. Out of that great vibration everything that is came into being.

"Vibration produces duality. To know the One Reality behind all appearances, remove yourself mentally from Nature's oppositional states. Accept with an even mind whatever comes to you in life: pleasure and pain, joy and sorrow, success and failure.

"Live for God alone. Serve Him only. Love only Him."

⊷ 11 ⊶

"Master," inquired a disciple, "what purpose does evil serve in God's creation? Surely the Lord is a God of goodness and love. Is it possible that, as certain modern writers claim, He doesn't know evil?"

Sri Yogananda chuckled. "God would have to be very stupid not to know evil! He, Who sees the fall of every sparrow, how could He not be aware of something so obvious?"

The disciple: "Perhaps He doesn't know it *as* evil."

Yogananda: "But the thing that makes it evil is the harm it does us. Certainly He is conscious that people are living in delusion, and that therefore they suffer. He Himself created this delusion."

The disciple: "Then did God create evil?"

Yogananda: "Evil is His *maya*, or cosmic illusion. It is a conscious force which, once brought into existence, seeks self-perpetuation. *Maya* is Satan. It tries to keep our consciousness earthbound. God, the One Reality, keeps trying at the same time to draw us back to Himself, by His divine love."

The disciple: "But then it must have been meant for Satan to play a role in the divine scheme of things."

Yogananda, smiling: "Evil serves the same purpose as does the villain in a drama. The villain's misdeeds help to awaken in us love for the hero and for virtuous ways. Similarly, evil and its painful after-effects are meant to awaken in us love for goodness and God."

The disciple: "But Master, if good and evil are both merely parts of a cosmic drama, what does it matter what roles we play in the story? Whether as saints or as gangsters, our parts will be illusory, and won't affect our true nature as images of God."

The Master laughed. "You are right in the ultimate sense. But don't forget that, if you play the part of a villain in a drama, in that drama you will also have to receive the villain's punishment!

"If, on the other hand, you play the role of a saint, you will awaken from this cosmic dream, and enjoy oneness with the Dreamer for all eternity."

⊸ 12 ⊷

The Master, addressing a new disciple: "What keeps the earth from shooting out into space, away from the sun?"

"The sun's gravitational pull, Sir," replied the disciple.

"Then what keeps the earth from being drawn back into the sun?"

"The earth's centrifugal force, which pulls it constantly outward, away from that center."

The Master, with an inward smile, dropped the subject. Months later, the disciple realized that his guru had been speaking metaphorically of God as the sun, Who draws all things back to Himself, and of man as the earth, ever trying to escape the pull of God's love while chasing after worldly desires.

Paramhansa Yogananda was hinting that one should not resist with worldly restlessness the pull of divine love on his soul.

1   Genesis 1:2.
2   Genesis 1:2.

Chapter 4

THE SOUL AND GOD

–⇥ 1 ⇤–

"God is the ocean of Spirit, and human beings are like waves that rise and fall on the ocean's surface.

"From a rowboat, the waves appear endlessly varied. Some are large and threatening; others, small and easy to row upon. From an airplane, however, all that is seen is the ocean itself, not the waves on its surface.

"Even so, to one who is absorbed in the play of *maya*— attached to success, and fearful of failure; attached to good health, and fearful of illness; attached to earthly existence, and fearful of death—the waves of human experience appear real and endlessly varied. To the man of non-attachment, however, all is Brahma: All is God.

"The greater a storm, the higher the waves on the ocean. Even so, the more violent the storm of delusion in a person's mind, the more he exalts himself above others and affirms his independence both of man and of God.

"Can anyone ever escape his Creator? We are all a part of God, even as waves are a part of the ocean. Our separateness from Him is an appearance, merely.

"When people affirm their individuality, and thereby raise themselves up in vanity and pride, they crash aggressively against other ego-waves, whipped up, like them, by delusion's storm. Like ocean waves in a tempest, they heave and toss about, conquering one minute, being conquered the next, in a ceaseless frenzy of conflict and competition.

"In a storm, the surface of the ocean knows no peace. Similarly, as long as the storm of delusion rages in the human mind, a person knows no peace, but only tension and anxiety.

"Peace comes when the storm is stilled, whether outwardly in Nature, or inwardly in a person's consciousness. As the storm of *maya* subsides, the wave of the ego subsides also. As the devotee's ego diminishes, he relaxes and accepts once again his connection with the infinite Spirit.

"Spiritually developed people no longer vie together, but splash about happily, in cheerful harmony with one another, with Nature, and with God."

⋯⊷ 2 ⊶⋯

A certain person had superficially studied the *Vedanta* philosophy of India with its teaching, "All is Brahma." Thereafter he went about proudly declaring to one and all, "I am God!" When this boast was reported to Paramhansa Yogananda, the Master laughed.

"People are so skillful in their ignorance! It is not the teaching of *Vedanta* to make such a cosmic statement in ego-consciousness. The ocean may rightly say, 'I am the waves that dance on my surface.' But has the wave a right to say, 'I am the ocean'? Absurd!

"Become one, first, with the ocean of God. If in that consciousness you declare, 'I am He,' it won't be as the little wave that you are speaking, but as the ocean itself. Your sense of 'I,' then, won't be limited by the ego.

"Better still even so is it to say, 'The ocean has become this little wave of a body,' lest people misunderstand the level from which you are speaking."

⋯⊷ 3 ⊶⋯

"God is the electricity, and human beings are the light bulbs. The bulbs may be infinitely varied in shape, color, and brightness. The actual power with which they shine, however, is the same for all.

"People are tricked by appearances. They say, 'What a beautiful person! What lovely hair! See the brightness of her smile!'

"When the electricity is turned off in a room, where is the color and brightness of the light bulb?

"Never forget the true Source of power in yourself, and in all that you see around you."

—4—

"Human beings are like the individual jets of flame on a gas stove. God is the reservoir of gas underneath.

"The larger the opening of a jet, the stronger also the flame. Even so, the more we open ourselves to God's presence within us, the greater the light and power that He can manifest in our lives.

"Again, the smaller the opening of a gas jet, the weaker the flame. Even so, the more we close ourselves off from God, through pride and through indifference to the needs of others, the weaker the flame of power and inspiration in our lives.

"A clogged opening may not even ignite at all, even though a little of the gas still manages to leak through it. Many people, similarly, are so lacking in inner vitality that the most one can say of them is that they exist; they are not, properly speaking, *alive.* These are the kind of people to whom Jesus referred when he said, 'Let the dead bury their dead.'"[1]

—5—

"Visualize many pots filled with water, standing in a garden. Then imagine the moon shining down from above.

In every pot, the moon's reflection will appear separate. In fact, however, all the pots reflect the same moon.

"That is how God is in the souls of men. Though reflected in every human being, He is forever untainted by human consciousness. Even if you broke all the pots, the moon's light would remain the same.

"Wise is he who, beholding the light of life shining in his little 'pot' of human consciousness, looks up to its origins in the 'moon' above—in God. But foolish, he who becomes engrossed in the moon in its reflection. When the pot breaks, what will he have left?"

6

"The Hindu teachings," Yogananda said, "are pantheistic. Christian thinkers have twisted this fact into a denunciation of Hinduism. Their error lies in thinking pantheism means worshiping God *as* everything, instead of *as expressed in* everything.

"Isn't it much sweeter to see His manifestations everywhere: His beauty in the sunset; His tears for human error in the rain; His tenderness expressed in a mother's love for her baby? If God is omnipresent, isn't it obvious that He must also be *in* everything? We must seek Him behind His veils.

"Even a veil, however, may suggest the form it hides. All things in creation, for those who love God, remind them of Him.

"Above all, remember, as Jesus said, 'The kingdom of God is within *you*.'"[2]

━▶ 7 ◀━

"What is the ego?" asked a devotee.

"The ego," Paramhansa Yogananda replied, "is the soul attached to the body."

━▶ 8 ◀━

"Like waves on the ocean, human beings play for a time, caught by the storm of delusion. The ocean, however, is all the time pulling, pulling. Sooner or later, all of them will have to be drawn back, to merge at last into the vast Ocean of Divine Love from which they came."

━▶ 9 ◀━

"Self-realization means realizing your true Self as the great ocean of Spirit, by breaking the delusion that you are this little ego, this little human body and personality."

1   Matthew 8:22.
2   Luke 17:21.

Chapter 5

ONE GOD, ONE RELIGION

→•◦ 1 ◦•←

"An elephant driver had six sons, all of them blind. One day he gave them the job of washing his elephant. When the brothers had completed the task, they began discussing what manner of animal was the elephant.

"'Easy!' said one. 'The elephant is a couple of large bones.' He'd been washing the tusks.

"'How can you say such a thing?' remonstrated another. 'The elephant is like a thick rope.' He'd been washing the trunk.

"The third son insisted that the elephant was like a couple of fans. He'd been washing the ears.

"To the fourth son, the elephant resembled four pillars. He'd been washing the legs.

"The fifth son had been washing the sides. He described the elephant as a wall that breathed.

"The sixth and last cried, 'You boys can't fool me! I *know*. My own experience has revealed to me that the elephant is a little piece of string hanging down from the sky.' He'd been washing the tail.

"As each son expressed his own opinion more insistently, there developed a heated argument. After some time, the father walked in and heard them shouting at one another. Listening to this swelling tide of bigotry, he cried, laughing, 'My sons, you are all fighting over nothing!'

"'Nothing?' one of them shouted. 'My brothers are all liars, and here they have the audacity to call *me* one!'

"'My dear children,' said the father placatingly, 'each of you has washed only a part of the elephant, but I alone have seen it in its entirety. It is everything that each of you says it is, but,' he added, 'it is also much more than any of you suspect.'

"He went on to describe to them what the elephant really looked like. 'So you see, my sons,' he finished, 'you are all right—but you are also all wrong!'

"Such is the case with God," concluded Sri Yogananda, "and with the approaches to Him that are taken by the different religions. God is One, but the paths to Him are many. Countless, too, are the ways in which He may be experienced, and described."

⇢⊸2⊷⇠

"Here in the West, people speak of Hindus as heathens. But did you know that in India people describe Christians as heathens? Ignorance, I say, is fifty-fifty the world over.

"The wise, however, see God everywhere—even in those who don't know Him at all."

⇢⊸3⊷⇠

"The true basis of religion is not belief, but intuitive experience. *Intuition is the soul's power of knowing God.* To know what religion is really all about, one must know God."

⇢⊸4⊷⇠

"Faith is different from belief. Faith is rooted in experience. Belief is provisional faith.

"Belief is necessary in the beginning. Without it, people wouldn't trouble to seek God. Mere belief, however, is not enough. When people remain satisfied with their beliefs, their religion becomes dogmatic, and therefore closed to further growth.

"I say, make spiritual practice, not belief, your 'dogma.' Don't remain satisfied even with regular meditation, until you have found God."

--•5•--

"The true custodians of religion are the saints and masters—those, in other words, who commune with God. It is not enough to study the scriptures and become a D.D., or, 'Doctor of Divinity.' (Whenever I see those letters, I think, 'Doctor of Delusion'!) By contrast, many saints have been illiterate. One who knows the truth in his soul, however, understands more than any theologian whose knowledge is derived from mere book-learning and dry intellectual discourses.

"'Suffer little children to come unto me,' said Jesus, 'for of such is the kingdom of God.'"[1]

--•6•--

"A donkey may carry a burden of Bibles and other holy writings on its back. Does it thereby become spiritual? More likely, the very weight of all those books will merely deprive it of any peace it may have had when it was carrying nothing!"

⊷7⊶

"Why is it that out of one Bible so many churches have
arisen, and so many diverse opinions about Truth? Each
Christian sect offers a different interpretation of what Jesus
meant. Why?

"The answer is that people's understanding is limited. They
cannot imagine anything except in terms of their own experience. Instead of trying to discover that part of themselves
which is made in God's image, they seek to cast God in their
own human image!

"A person walking through narrow city lanes sees only
the walls hemming him in on either side. He cannot see the
gardens behind them. From an airplane, however, one sees
beyond the walls, beyond the gardens, beyond the very
confines of the city—beyond even the horizon of those
who, while not hemmed in by walls, yet remain standing on
solid earth."

⊷8⊶

"Better a truth stated by one saint than a dogma avowed by
millions.

"The numbers of a religion's adherents don't guarantee
its validity. Never accept an idea merely because it has won
popular approval. Be qualitative, not quantitative, in your
approach to truth if you would achieve that understanding of
it which alone, Jesus said, can make you free."

9

"Sectarianism is anathema to religion. Only shallow people think, 'Mine is the one, true way. All other ways are false.'

"There is a story that when Billy Sunday, the famous revivalist preacher, died, St. Peter wouldn't let him enter the 'pearly gates.'

"'What do you mean, you won't let me in?' demanded the revivalist, outraged.

"'What did you do during your lifetime on earth to come close to God?' St. Peter inquired.

"'Why, what about all those thousands of sinners I converted and sent to heaven?'

"'You may have sent them,' St. Peter replied, 'but none have arrived.'"

10

"Science and religion should work hand in hand together. From religion, science can learn a more intuitive approach to reality: experiential, rather than only experimental. And from science, religion can learn to depend more on common sense—to be more reasonable, and less dogmatic.

"Religionists should learn above all to test their beliefs, just as science does. Religious leaders should encourage people to prove the teachings of their faith in their own lives, and not to remain satisfied with the claims of others."

⊷11⊶

"How is it possible for a Christian to accept the truth of other religions?" queried an orthodox believer. "Jesus not only gave us a teaching: He also emphasized the uniqueness of that teaching. He stressed, moreover, his own uniqueness as the Son of God."

"The truth *is* unique, certainly," Yogananda replied. "For, whereas the ways of error are many, the way *out of* error is only one.

"There is but one way for the soul to go: It must go back to God. People's mistake lies in attaching a particular name to that way, and in insisting that that name alone be accepted by everyone.

"Look to the saints, rather than to priests and ministers, for the truth. Saints may be found in every religion. And fools and sinners, too, may be found everywhere.

"It wasn't the wise of other faiths that Jesus ever combated. It was the spiritual ignorance that he encountered among his own listeners!"

⊷12⊶

"'Are you saved?' an orthodox preacher once demanded of me. Saved from what? I wondered. Finding me unwilling to join him in his narrow interpretation of the truth, he shouted at me angrily, 'You will go to hell!'

"Well, what is hell if not the torment of harmful emotions such as anger? Smiling, I replied, 'I may get there by and by, but *you*, my friend, are there already!'

"Other people had been listening with keen interest to our conversation, which took place on a train. When I gave him that answer, they all laughed."

⊸ 13 ⊶

"Your beliefs won't save you."

⊸ 14 ⊶

"The Bible condemns idolatry," remarked a Christian visitor, "yet I've read that in every Hindu home there is at least one idol. How can Christians—and Jews, for that matter—fail to condemn this practice as heathen?"

The Master replied: "Suppose you see a little girl playing with a doll and treating it as though it were her baby. Will you scold her, saying, 'That doll is merely an inanimate object'? Playing with dolls can even serve the practical purpose of helping the child to prepare for motherhood someday.

"Images, similarly, can help people to awaken and focalize their devotion. Don't Christians keep images on their altars, too,—Jesus, for example, on the cross?

"Again, think of all the images that God has given us in Nature. If we love Him, doesn't the beauty of trees, flowers, and sunsets remind us of His infinite beauty?

"The idolatry condemned in the Bible is the ego's practice of placing the creation above the Creator: of worshiping money, and not the divine treasure within the Self; of worshiping human love, and not divine love; of worshiping false intoxicants, such as wine and sex, and not praying for the 'intoxication' of divine ecstasy."

⟶ 15 ⟵

"The Bible," objected a newcomer to Paramhansa Yogananda's work, "tells us that Jesus is the only Son of God. How, then, can you speak of other masters as his equal?"

The Master replied: "When the Jews accused Jesus of blasphemy for saying, 'I and my Father are one,' he answered them, 'Don't your scriptures say, *you* are gods?'[2]

"The followers of every religion like to claim uniqueness for their own beliefs. Their claim, however, stems from human misunderstanding and ignorance. Everyone likes to claim that his own possessions, too, are the best!

"Jesus, like all great masters, spoke from two levels of identity: the human and the divine. As a human being, he could cry out on the cross, 'Father, why hast Thou forsaken me?' But in his infinite, divine Self, he could rightly say he was the only Son of God. For in that consciousness he was identified with the Christ consciousness, which is the only reflection in all creation of God, the Father beyond creation.

"The Christ consciousness is not a man with a beard and a flowing white robe! When Jesus used the pronoun 'I,' speaking from that vast state of consciousness, he was referring to the infinite Self of all beings, not to his little human body.

"The Christ consciousness underlies the entire created universe. Anyone who withdraws his consciousness from attachment to the ego and unites it with Infinity can with perfect right say with Jesus, 'I am the Son of God.'

"He can say, too, 'I and my Father are one,' just as Jesus did, since the Son and the Father are aspects of the same reality.

"In that state, his sense of 'I' is no longer limited by the human body. The wave has merged back into the vast ocean from which it came. It has *become* the ocean."

⟶ 16 ⟵

"You say that the goal of life is to find God," challenged a student of comparative religions. "Yet this belief is not universally held. The Buddhists, for example, don't even believe in God."

Yogananda replied: "Buddha was no atheist. His teachings, however, like those of every great master, had to offer correction to the misconceptions of his day. The people at that time were prone to let God do the work for them, spiritually speaking. Buddha therefore stressed the importance of man's own effort in the spiritual search.

"As the saying goes, 'The proof of the pudding is in the eating.' Those who deeply practice Buddha's teachings, and not those who merely argue about them, achieve their goal. Achieving it, they find it to be the same as that of all the great religions: realization of the infinite Self, and freedom from the trammels of delusion.

"As for seeking agreement among all religions in the world," the Master continued, "it would be a mistake to suppose that all of them derive equally from the same level of divine insight."

⟶ 17 ⟵

"The truths underlying religion are eternal. They cannot be invented. From their source in the realization of God-enlightened masters, they become diluted by their contact with unenlightened human beings.

"That is why God from time to time sends His awakened sons back to earth, to revive the spirit of religion and to return the timeless teachings to their pristine purity.

"There will always be differences of emphasis, according to the varying needs of the times. The fundamental truths, however, remain forever the same."

⇥18⇤

A student: "What is the special purpose of your mission on earth?"

Yogananda: "To awaken people to their need for Self-realization, through meditation, and through keeping good company, or fellowship, with other truth-seeking souls.

"Hence the name of this organization, Self-Realization Fellowship. SRF was sent to bring back to the world the original teachings and science of yoga as taught by Krishna, and the original Christianity of Jesus Christ."

⇥19⇤

A visitor: "Is your teaching a new religion?"

The Master: "It is a new *expression* of truths that are eternal."

⤜20⤛

The great religions of the world have always been brought by *avatars*—incarnations, or "descents" of God. Such an incarnation was Krishna. Such also were Jesus and Buddha. An *avatar* is a fully liberated master who returns to earth to fulfill a special divine mission.

This disciple once asked Paramhansa Yogananda, "Master, are you an *avatar*?"

With quiet simplicity the Master replied, "A work of this importance would have to have been started by such a one.

1   Matthew 19:14.
2   John 10:34.

Chapter 6

THE LAW OF LIFE

-→▨ 1 ▨←-

"There is a fundamental law of life. Recognizing it, we understand where life comes from, and where it is heading. To discover it, look beyond people's immediate goals to what they aim finally to accomplish in their lives. Consider life's ultimate destiny: in other words, its highest potential for development.

"Life, as seen through the eyes of worldly people, seems infinitely complex. Mankind is driven by countless desires, and seeks their fulfillment in innumerable ways. Certain fundamental drives there are, however, that are universal to mankind and to creatures everywhere.

"Charles Darwin identified the first of these drives. Life, he declared, is a ceaseless struggle for survival. His statement, however, is incomplete. Survival *is* one of life's fundamental instincts, certainly, but survival for what? Survival in a state of coma? Surely not! Consciousness, too, is a need universally felt. Living creatures not only want to exist: They want to be conscious of their existence.

"A third drive must be added, without which even perpetual, conscious existence would be incomplete. For if a creature experiences too much suffering for too long, may it not prefer death to continued consciousness or existence? Living beings want to be conscious of their existence, but they also want consciously to *enjoy* that existence.

"The fundamental instinct of life, then, may be summed up thus: as *a desire for continued, conscious existence in a state of perpetual enjoyment.* For 'continued existence' we may substitute the word, 'immortality.'

"Thus do all beings reveal their divine nature. For this is what God is: *ever-existing, ever-conscious, ever-new bliss*— or *satchidananda*, as Swami Shankaracharya defined Him many centuries ago.[1] God may be defined in countless ways:

as infinite Light, Power, Wisdom, and so forth. The most meaningful definition of all, however, in terms of life's most fundamental drives, is *satchidananda*.

"The law of life refers to the basic impulse, underlying all other desires, for *satchidananda*. Every living being is governed by this impulse.

"The deep-seated craving for eternal bliss manifests itself, first, in the constant effort of all creatures to avoid pain; and second, in their ceaseless struggle to find happiness, or joy.

"Complexities arise because soul-joy is forgotten, and because people substitute for it the fleeting pleasures of the senses. All things, however, came from Bliss, or God. Eventually, all things must evolve back to that Bliss-state."

⸰⸱ 2 ⸱⸰

A visitor: "Doesn't it seem a bit trivial to define God as joy, and to equate man's quest for Him with the search for happiness? Duty, surely, is more important than the desire for personal fulfillment. And God is such a grand concept that I can't really imagine Him as a kind of exaltation of joy.

"I read somewhere once of the 'wonderful solemnity' of a life lived in the presence of God. I confess I find this a much more satisfying concept."

Paramhansa Yogananda replied: "Would you like to live in this 'wonderful solemnity' for all eternity?"

"Well, I can't really imagine eternity," admitted the visitor. "But no, I suppose I'd expect something more."

Yogananda: "You see? We must seek God with longing, with devotion. And how can we long for something that isn't deeply meaningful to us?

"People," he added, "hold God at a distance when they regard Him with too much awe. They go to church as a solemn duty, and wear long faces as if attending a funeral. The truth is, finding God is the funeral of all sorrows!

"Before our Heavenly Father we should be like little children. He likes that. He has enough awesome responsibilities in running this universe! He owns everything. He knows everything. He is all-powerful. The only thing lacking to Him is our love. That is what God wants from us: our love; our trust in Him; our joy in His infinite joy.

"He doesn't need from us carefully contrived theological definitions. And He doesn't want prayers that are chiseled to perfection lest they give offense to His imperial ears. He wants us to love Him in all simplicity, just like children."

3

A man burdened with worldly responsibilities asked, "What place does duty hold on the path to inner joy?"

Sri Yogananda replied: "To live irresponsibly is to live for the ego, not for God. The greater a person's emphasis on ego-fulfillment, the less his awareness of true joy.

"To fulfill one's duties in life may not be easy, and it may not always be immediately enjoyable. Attaining divine joy is a long-term proposition. Man must discharge his duties in life, and not avoid them, if he would attain freedom in eternity."

--⊷4⊶--

"What is evil?" asked a devotee.

"Evil," replied Yogananda, "is the absence of true joy. That is what makes it evil, you see. Otherwise, can you say that a tiger commits evil in killing its prey? To kill is the tiger's nature, given to it by God. Nature's laws are impersonal.

"Evil comes into the picture when one has the potential for attaining inner joy. Anything that separates us from that divine state of being is evil for us, because it distances our awareness from that which we really are, and from that which we really want in life.

"Hence the scriptural injunctions against lust, for example, and pride. The commandments are for man's welfare, not for the Lord's gratification! They are warnings to the unwary, that, although certain attitudes and actions may at first seem fulfilling, the end of the road for anyone pursuing them is not happiness, but pain."

--⊷5⊶--

"The law of life is designed to teach us how to live in harmony with objective Nature and with our true, inner nature.

"If you touch your fingers to a hot stove, they will be burned. The pain you feel will be a warning, put there by Nature to protect you from injuring your body.

"And if you treat others unkindly, you will receive unkindness in return, both from others and from life. Your own heart, moreover, will grow shriveled and dry. Thus does Nature warn people that by unkindness they do violence to their attunement with the inner Self.

"When we know what the law is and conduct ourselves accordingly, we live in lasting happiness, good health, and perfect harmony with ourselves and with all life."

–⊷6⊶–

"If we are God's children, and He loves us, why does He allow us to suffer?"

To this frequently asked question, the Master once replied: "Suffering is a reminder that this world is not our home. If it were perfect for us, how many people would seek a better one? Even with things as imperfect as they are, see how few people seek God! Out of a thousand, said Krishna, perhaps one.

"The law of life is this: The less one lives in harmony with the truth within, the more he suffers; but the more he lives in harmony with that truth, the more he experiences unending happiness. Nothing then can touch him, even though his body waste away with disease and people ridicule and persecute him. Through all the vagaries of life, he remains ever blissfully centered in the indwelling Self."

–⊷7⊶–

"I once met a saint in India who had a very materialistic wife. Ordinarily, for a devotee, such a wife would pose a severe challenge. But this saint told me humorously, 'I have fooled her. She doesn't know where I am!' What he meant was, her scoldings couldn't touch the inner peace that he felt in God.

"Even great outward hardship cannot touch you, once you have learned to dwell always in the Self within."

⟿ 8 ⟾

A disciple, bothered one day by a host of gnats and flies while working in the hermitage garden, exclaimed in exasperation, "Master, why must the peace of these grounds be disturbed by such pests?"

With a smile the Master replied, "That is God's way of keeping us always moving toward Him."

⟿ 9 ⟾

A congregation member of one of the Self-Realization Fellowship churches came to Paramhansa Yogananda troubled by doubt. "Master," she said, "some people claim that, with so much suffering in the world, it is wrong for anyone to be happy. Doesn't personal enjoyment imply a lack of compassion for the sufferings of others?

"Jesus," she added, "is often depicted as a 'man of sorrows.' I've never heard him described as a man of joy."

Paramhansa Yogananda replied: "The Jesus I know is bliss-filled, not sorrowful! He grieves for the sorrows of mankind, yes, but his grief doesn't make him grief-stricken.

"Were he actually to embrace others' sorrows, what would he have to give them, except an increase of their misery?

"God's bliss makes those who have it compassionate for the millions who have missed the point of their existence. But compassion only adds to their inner bliss; it doesn't diminish it. For bliss is the cure all men are seeking, whether consciously or unconsciously. It is not a side issue, unrelated to suffering. The more blissful one feels within, the more he longs to share his bliss with all.

"Divine joy comes with self-expansion. Suffering, on the other hand, is the fruit of selfishness, of a contractive ego. Joy awakens compassion in the heart. It makes one long to infuse divine bliss into those who are weeping in sorrow."

1 "Existence-consciousness-bliss." Paramhansa Yogananda, though not claiming to do so, gave a fuller interpretation than one finds in standard texts on the subject. For the eternal nature of this state is not normally emphasized, though it is, of course, assumed. It is important to emphasize this point, however, since the term, *satchidananda*, was coined in order to show how God's nature corresponds to the most fundamental impulses of life.

Yogananda's definition of *ananda*, furthermore, as a bliss that is *ever-new* completes the picture by contrasting divine with earthly enjoyment, which forever ends in boredom and satiety.—*ed.*

Chapter 7

SIN IS IGNORANCE

→◉ 1 ◉←

"What is sin?" asked a disciple.

"Sin is error; it is born of ignorance," replied the Master.

"What is ignorance? What is error?"

"Ignorance is the lack of awareness of soul realities, and the substitution of this dream of delusion for those realities. Error is any action that is based on that misconception."

"Does not sin also mean breaking God's commandments?" inquired the disciple.

"Yes," replied Yogananda. "But ask yourself this: Why did God give mankind those commandments? It wasn't arbitrarily. And it certainly wasn't to keep us from finding happiness. Rather, it was to warn us that certain kinds of behavior will strengthen delusion's hold on our minds, and deprive us of true happiness.

"If one thinks of sin as breaking God's commandments, the thought then arises of God's anger and stern judgment. But the Lord is our very own! We are His children. Why should He judge us? It is we, rather, who judge ourselves when we imagine that anything we do is beyond forgiveness. But if we understand sin as error, we realize that our errors can be rectified."

Referring then to his own guru, Paramhansa Yogananda continued, "Sri Yukteswar used to say, as I wrote in *Autobiography of a Yogi*, 'Forget the past. The vanished lives of all men are dark with many shames. Human conduct is ever unreliable until man is anchored in the Divine. Everything in future will improve if you are making a spiritual effort now.'[1]

"I always like to remind people of this simple truth: *A saint is a sinner who never gave up!*"

—⊷ 2 ⊷—

"Why is murder a sin? Because the life that is in you is the same as the life in all beings. To deny anyone the right to live is to deny the reality of that universal life of which you, too, are an expression. Spiritually speaking, then, murder is suicide.

"Why is it sinful to steal? Because what you deny others you deny also yourself, in them, since the Self of others is also your own greater Self. The thief invariably, in the end, impoverishes himself. By emphasizing selfish desires above the realization of his universal Self, he cuts himself off from the one true Source of life and of all abundance. By taking from others for selfish gain, he narrows his own self-identity instead of, as he believes, expanding it.

"Giving of oneself to others, on the other hand, broadens that identity, and opens one to the unfailing Source of abundance.

"Why is it sinful to tell lies? Because by untruthfulness one cuts oneself off from reality, and from that higher truth which alone, as Jesus said, 'shall make you free.'2 By telling lies, one isolates oneself from the support which the universe offers freely and lovingly to all who would live in harmony with its laws.

"The liar destroys the foundation of everything he tries to accomplish in this world. His turns out, finally, to be a house built on sand. The simple words of a man of truth, on the other hand, are binding on the universe.

"And why is lustfulness a sin? Because lust is counterfeit love. It takes one in the opposite direction from the fulfillment that is found in true love. True love is divine. It is self-giving, never selfish.

"The lustful man, in seeking his own pleasure of others, loses power, even while deluding himself that he is gaining it.

He cuts himself off from soul-joy, even while imagining that he has attained the happiness he craves. He succeeds only, in the end, in creating disharmony within himself and in others.

"Harmony is the way of love. Disharmony is the way of self-affirmation. The lustful person loses his health, his peace of mind, and the very fulfillment he imagines himself to be finding. He becomes increasingly tired and nervous, and grows prematurely old, all because he denied divine love, the source of true and lasting well-being.

"And so is it with every sin. Sin is a denial of one's own deeper nature—of that Infinite Life which is the underlying reality of all beings."

3

"A man walking in a part of the country where diamonds had been discovered came upon an area that was littered with little pieces of broken glass, all shining in the sunlight.

"'Diamonds!' he thought excitedly. Stooping down to pick one of them up, he found that it was only a sliver of glass. Disappointed, he threw it away and reached for another. But it, too, proved to be only glass. And so he went on picking up one piece of glass after another. Sometimes he cut himself on the sharp edges. Every piece he tried proved as illusory as the first.

"Such is the way of sin. Its false glitter is attractive, but on experience it turns out to be nothing but 'broken glass.' Often it cuts the one who indulges in it. Always it proves disappointing.

"Sense pleasures can only end in satiety, anguishing monotony, and disgust. Why? For the simple reason that your physical senses are not your true Self."

4

"It is easy to sin. The effects of sin, however, are not so easy to dismiss. After peeling garlic, one's hands smell. It may take a lot of washing to rid them of that odor.

"Still, the odor *can* be washed away. So also can sin, through meditation, prayer, and right action, and by the grace of God. On this point never doubt. All your sins *must* be washed away at last.

"Still, why do in the first place that which in the end, and with a great deal of effort on your part, will only have to be undone?"

5

"When desires trouble the mind, always remind yourself of this truth: 'When ecstasy comes, everything goes.'"

6

"Never identify yourself with the errors you have committed. You are God's child. Claim your eternal relationship with Him."

7

"The worst sin is to call yourself a sinner. For in that very thought you open the door, and invite sin to enter your mind."

8

"To define yourself in terms of your human limitations is a desecration of the image of God within you."

9

"Never dwell on the thought of your shortcomings. Recall, instead, the memory of the good things you have done, and of the goodness that exists in the world. Convince yourself of your own innate perfection. Thus you will find yourself drawn to remember your eternal nature as a child of God."

10

"A room may be in darkness for thousands of years, but if a light is brought into it, in that very instant the darkness vanishes.

"So is it with sin. You cannot drive sin out of the mind any more than you can beat darkness out of a room with a stick. By concentration on delusion, indeed, you may only increase its hold on your mind. Bring in the light of God, however, through deep meditation and devotion, and the darkness will vanish as though it had never been."

11

Paramhansa Yogananda said, "Often, among churchgoing Christians, one hears the cry, 'We are all sinners!' (One almost wonders if that isn't a boast!)

"You know, there is a distinction between Christianity and what I call, 'Churchianity.' Christianity is the original teaching of Jesus. 'Churchianity' is what his followers have made of that teaching. Jesus Christ was crucified once, but his teachings have been crucified daily since then by millions who claimed to be Christians.

"Why think of yourself as a sinner? Oh, it may be all right sometimes, in the name of humility, provided your attention is focused on the greatness of God and not on your meanness before Him. But why dwell on negativity and limitation?

"If you want to find something valuable that has been buried under a mud slide, won't you be thinking of that object even as you dig through the mud? If you concentrated only on the mud, you might lose sight of your very purpose in digging, and abandon the search."

12

"Never count your faults. Just see that your love for God is deeply sincere. For God doesn't mind your imperfections: He minds your indifference."

⟶⊸ 13 ⊷⟵

"If you covered a gold image with a black cloth, would you then say that the image had become black? Of course not! You would know that, behind the veil, the image was still gold.

"So will it be when you tear away the black veil of ignorance which now hides your soul. You will behold again the unchanging beauty of your own divine nature."

⟶⊸ 14 ⊷⟵

"I once attended a service conducted by a certain well-known woman evangelist. During her sermon she suddenly cried out, 'You are all sinners! Get down on your knees!' I gazed around me. In all that large congregation I was the only one who wasn't kneeling. For I wouldn't accept the thought that I was a sinner!"

⟶⊸ 15 ⊷⟵

"Give to God not only the good that you do, but also the bad. I do not mean that you should deliberately do things that are wrong. But when you cannot help yourself, because of habits that are too strong, tell your mind that God is performing those actions through you.

"It is He, after all, who has dreamed your existence. You have merely hypnotized yourself with the thought of your weaknesses. If you make the Lord responsible for them, it will help you to break the false hold they have on your imagination. You'll find it easier, then, to recognize in yourself the perfect image of God."

⊷16⊷

"Never be afraid of God. Tell Him the things you've done wrong. Remind Him that you are His child. That is much better than whining, 'Lord, I am a sinner! I am a sinner!' You are made in His image. Pray, then, 'Well, Lord, I have made mistakes. If you want to beat me, all right. But once I know You, there can be no more temptation for me.'

"Put it to Him plainly. We didn't ask to be created. We didn't ask for temptation. A great saint in India used to pray, 'Lord, it wasn't my wish that You create me, but since You have done so, You have to release me!' Talk to Him that way, though always lovingly. Then at last, no matter what your faults, He will have to cleanse you of your imperfections, and take you back home where you belong."

⊷17⊷

"The simple thought that we are not free is what keeps us from being free. If we could break even that one idea, we would go into *samadhi*.[3]

"*Samadhi* is not something we have to acquire. We have it already. Just think: Eternally we have been with God; for a short time we are in delusion; then again we are free in Him forever!"

"Sir," asked a disciple, "if I said I was free, I wouldn't be, would I?"

"Oh, yes!"

The Master then added with a wry smile, "But you answered your own question. You said, 'I wouldn't be!'"

⊷18⊶

Though filled with compassion for all, Paramhansa Yogananda could also be very stern on the subject of sin when the occasion demanded it.

A certain young woman in Chicago had contracted syphilis from her boyfriend. To avenge herself on him and on all men, she sought to tempt and infect every man she met.

Having been granted an interview with the Master, she smiled at him alluringly and said, "You are very nice."

"Sin and disease!" scoffed the Master, gazing at her scornfully. The woman burst into tears. Then she confessed her story.

After she'd promised him never to behave like that again, the Master healed her and sent her on her way.

⊷19⊶

"I am sorry for those who are ill," the Master said. "Why should I not be equally sorry for those who live in sin? They are ill spiritually."

⊷20⊶

"Spiritual ignorance is the greatest sin. It is what makes all other sins possible."

⇢⊷ 21 ⊷⇠

"A woman came up to me once and cried, 'You must be saved by the blood!'

"'Produce a quart,' I challenged her. She was flabbergasted.

"What do fanatics know of spiritual truths? They spout words like slogans, and shout themselves hoarse about 'the blood of Christ,' all the time living sinful lives themselves. Then they imagine that calling themselves sinners will 'get them off the hook.'

"If they want Jesus Christ to save them, let them commune with him in inner silence. Let them 'receive him,' as the Bible says, in their souls. Only then will they be able to 'become the sons of God.'"[4]

⇢⊷ 22 ⊷⇠

"I heard a certain minister preach, and I'll never forget the way he drew his words out 'soulfully,' as he imagined, when urging people to accept 'the pi-i-u-u-u-ure Holy Ghost.' The words, 'Holy Ghost,' were uttered abruptly for dramatic emphasis.

"Such people are inspired not by the Holy Ghost, but by the 'unholy ghost' of emotions!"

—23—

"Is it good to go to confession?" asked an orthodox Christian.

"It may help, as a means of getting one to admit his faults to himself. For only by self-honesty can one deal with his shortcomings effectively.

"It is always better, however, to confess your faults to a man or woman of wisdom. Only such a person can really help you. Otherwise, you may receive bad advice.

"As Jesus said, 'If the blind lead the blind, they both end up in a ditch.'[5] Confession to a saint is good, but not always to someone who is unenlightened spiritually.

"With God, however, be always frank and open. From Him you should conceal nothing."

"Aren't priests," his questioner persevered, "empowered to forgive sins?"

"To forgive sin," replied Yogananda, "is to heal a person of the consequences of sin.[6] Find out if they can 'forgive' you the sin, for example, of overeating. Will they be able to cure you of your subsequent stomach ache?"

⇾⊷24⊷⇽

"Never mind if you have erred. Just call to God with trust-
ing love. Hide nothing from Him. He knows all your faults,
far better than you do! Be completely open with Him.

"You may find it helpful to pray to God as your Divine
Mother. For the Mother aspect of God is all-merciful. Pray,
'Divine Mother, naughty or good, I am Thy child. Thou *must*
release me!'

"Even the human mother loves her naughty children as
much as her good ones. Sometimes she loves them even more,
for their need is greater.

"Don't be afraid of your Divine Mother. Sing to Her in this
way from your heart: 'Receive me on Thy lap, O Mother!
Cast me not at death's door.'"[7]

⇾⊷25⊷⇽

"God loves you just as much as He loves Krishna, Jesus,
and the other great masters. You are a drop of the same ocean
of Spirit. For the ocean is made up of all its drops. You are
a part of God. You were given your importance by the Lord
Himself. You are His very own."

⇾⊷26⊷⇽

"Always dwell on the thought of your innate perfection
in God. Gold is still gold, though it lie buried under the
accumulated filth of ages."

—27—

"The Lord wants to take us out of this terrible turmoil of life. That is the only thing He desires for us. For He loves each one of us. He does not want us to suffer. His interest in our salvation is personal, and full of mercy."

—28—

"A certain man was dying of diabetes. The doctors had given him only three months to live. He decided, 'If all that I have left to me is three months, let me spend them in seeking God.'

"Gradually he disciplined himself to sit in meditation for longer and longer periods every day. And all the while he kept praying, 'Lord, come into this broken temple.'

"Three months passed, and he was still alive. A year passed. Continuing his intense prayer, he gradually increased his time of meditation to eighteen hours a day.

"Two more years passed.

"After three years, suddenly a great light filled his being. He was caught up in ecstasy. On returning from that divine state, he found that his body had been healed.

"'Lord,' he prayed, 'I didn't ask for a healing. All I asked was that You come to me.'

"And the voice of the Lord answered, 'Where My light is, there no darkness can dwell.'

"The saint then wrote with his finger on the sand, 'And on this day the Lord came into my broken temple, and made it whole!'"

1 *Autobiography of a Yogi,* Chapter 12, "Years in My Master's Hermitage," Self-Realization Fellowship, Los Angeles, California.

2 John 8:32.

3 The state of oneness with Cosmic consciousness.

4 John 1:12.

5 Matthew 15:14.

6 "And while he was proclaiming the message to them, a man was brought who was paralysed. Four men were carrying him, but because of the crowd they could not get him near. So they opened up the roof over the place where Jesus was, and when they had broken through they lowered the stretcher on which the paralysed man was lying. When Jesus saw their faith, he said to the paralysed man, 'My son, your sins are forgiven.'

"Now there were some lawyers sitting there and they thought to themselves, 'Why does the fellow talk like that? This is blasphemy! Who but God alone can forgive sins?' Jesus knew in his own mind that this was what they were thinking, and said to them: 'Why do you harbour thoughts like these? Is it easier to say to this paralysed man, "Your sins are forgiven," or to say, "Stand up, take your bed, and walk"? But to convince you that the Son of Man has the right on earth to forgive sins'—he turned to the paralysed man—'I say to you, stand up, take your bed, and go home.' And he got up, took his stretcher at once, and went out in full view of them all, so that they were astounded and praised God. 'Never before,' they said, 'have we seen the like.'" (Mark 2:3–12)

7 A translation of the first lines of a Bengali song that the Master loved.

Chapter 8

The Law of Karma

-⊷ 1 ⊷-

A visitor: "The Bible says that evildoers shall be punished, and the good, rewarded. Do you subscribe to this teaching?"

Paramhansa Yogananda: "Certainly. If we accept the principle of cause and effect in Nature, and of action and reaction in physics, how can we not believe that this natural law extends also to human beings? Do not humans, too, belong to the natural order?

"This is the law of karma: As you sow, so shall you reap.[1] If you sow evil, you will reap evil in the form of suffering. And if you sow goodness, you will reap goodness in the form of inner joy."

The visitor: "How specific is the law? In physics, the law of motion states that for every action there is an *equal and opposite* reaction. In Nature, effects are often very specifically, and not only vaguely, related to their causes. Yet we've been taught to view reward and punishment for human behavior in more general terms. If we're good, we've been told, we'll go to heaven, and if we're bad, we'll go to hell. But people don't think of themselves as reaping specific consequences for specific deeds."

Yogananda: "The karmic law is exact. There is, furthermore, no question of suffering in hell for eternity. (How could the misdeeds of a few years on earth deserve eternal punishment? Could a finite cause have an infinite effect?)

"To understand karma, you must realize that thoughts are things. The very universe, in the final analysis, is composed not of matter but of consciousness. Matter responds, far more than most people realize, to the power of thought. For will power directs energy, and energy in turn acts upon matter. Matter, indeed, *is* energy.

"The stronger the will, the greater the force of energy—and the greater, consequently, the energy's impact on material events. A strong will, especially if combined with awareness of the cosmic energy, can effect miracles. It can cure diseases, and make a person well. It can ensure success in any undertaking. The very seasons are obedient to the man of strong will power and of deep faith.

"Even unenlightened human beings shape their destinies, more than they themselves realize, according to the way they use their power of will. For no action is ever an isolated event. Always, it invites from the universe a reaction that corresponds exactly to the type and the force of energy behind the deed.

"Action originates in the will, which directs energy toward its desired end. This, then, is the definition of will power: *desire plus energy, directed toward fulfillment.*

"Energy, like electricity, generates a magnetic field. And that magnetic field attracts to itself the consequences of action.

"The binding force between human action and cosmic reaction is the ego. The consciousness of ego ensures that a person's actions will have personal consequences for himself. These consequences may be delayed, if the will power engendering a thought or deed was not powerful enough to have immediate results, or if its thrust was thwarted by other, conflicting energies. Sooner or later, however, every action, whether of body, of thought, or of desire, must reap its final reaction. It is like a circle completing itself.

"Thus, man, made as he is in the image of God, becomes in his turn a creator.

"The results of good and bad deeds are not experienced only after death. Heaven and hell are realities even here on earth, where people reap the painful consequences of their folly, and the harmonious results of right action.

"People seldom think of their own actions as bad. Whatever they do seems, at least to them, well-intentioned. But if they create disharmony for others, and thus on deeper levels of their being for themselves, those waves of disharmony will inevitably return to them in the form of disharmony.

"Every action, every thought, reaps its own corresponding rewards.

"Human suffering is not a sign of God's anger with mankind. It is a sign, rather, of man's ignorance of the divine law.

"The law is forever infallible in its workings."

2

A disciple: "Master, is karma only individual, or does it affect also groups of people?"

Yogananda: "Karma is action, simply, whether physical or mental, whether individual or performed by a group, a nation, or a group of nations."

Disciple: "To what extent is an individual influenced by mass karma?"

Yogananda: "It all depends on the strength of his individual karma.

"In an air crash, for example, it needn't be that all who died in it had the karma to do so. The karma of the majority in that disaster may simply have been stronger than that of the minority to live.

"Those, however, with strong enough karma to live would be saved—either during the crash itself, or from taking that flight in the first place.

"The karma of a nation depends on the degree to which its people as a whole have acted in keeping with cosmic law.

"I have often said that America cannot lose in the long run, if her enemies attack her, because her karma is basically very good, despite a few wrong things she has done. The karma of

her present enemies, by contrast, is bad, and they shall have
to pay for it.

"Even animals create karma. Their consciousness,
however, including their consciousness of ego, is weak. Thus,
they are directed rather by mass than by individual karma."

→◉ 3 ◉←

A disciple: "Is it always bad karma to kill?"

The Master: "No. It depends on the intention behind
the act, and also on the over-all consequences. The soldier
who kills in conscious support of a righteous cause—for
example, in defending his country against invasion by a ruth-
less tyrant—incurs no bad karma. Rather, his action is good
karma."

Disciple: "What about the American soldiers in Korea.
What karma are they getting for shooting the enemy?"

The Master: "To fight in this cause is good karma, not bad
karma. For this is a holy war. The villain must be defeated, lest
the whole world, in the end, become enslaved."

→◉ 4 ◉←

A disciple: "Master, in *Autobiography of a Yogi* you
quoted Sri Yukteswar as saying, 'A man incurs the debt of
a minor sin if he is forced to kill an animal or any other living
thing.'[2] It must be wrong, then, to kill mosquitoes, flies, and
other such pests. Am I correct?"

Paramhansa Yogananda: "It is always better to kill
harmful creatures than to endanger human life."

The disciple: "But Sir, can one say that these insects are a danger to human life? Mostly they seem just a nuisance."

Paramhansa Yogananda: "Still, in those countries where they are allowed to thrive there is a high mortality rate owing to the diseases they spread. In countries where their proliferation is kept under control, there is much less filth and disease; consequently, people on an average live much longer. It is better, therefore, to keep the world free of such pests.

"Besides," Sri Yogananda added, "they are instruments of evil. Evil, too, must be kept under control."

⟿ 5 ⟾

"How many forms does karma take?" asked a devotee— thinking, perhaps, of the simple judgments meted out in a court of human law.

"You are confusing karma with punishment," the Master replied. Smilingly he added, "Many make that mistake. But karma means, simply, action.

"Action may be of many kinds, and may be intrinsically good, bad, or neutral, neutral action often serving as a transition between good and bad. The universe itself, according to the Hindu scriptures, is a mixture of three qualities, or *gunas* as they are called: the good, the activating, and the bad.

"The good quality, called *sattwa guna*, elevates the consciousness toward its source in God. The activating, *rajas* or *raja guna*, is only that: It impels people toward action for ego-benefit, though not necessarily toward bad action.

"The bad *guna* is called *tamas*. It is bad because it darkens the understanding.

"Most human beings are worldly. They act for personal gain. Few do so with a will to hurt others; few people are actually evil.

"The consequences of action are as multifarious as the deeds themselves.

"The Bible says, 'Whoso sheddeth man's blood, by man shall his blood be shed.'[3] That wasn't a commandment. It was an explanation of the divine law.

"Jesus told a man whom he'd healed, 'Sin no more, lest a worse thing come unto thee.'[4] The implication was clear: The man's disease was due to his having sinned in the first place.

"On the positive side, think of people who succeed effortlessly at anything they attempt to do. (At least, their success may appear effortless.) Whence came their good fortune? It was, quite simply, good karma."

The devotee: "Still, many a murderer has died peacefully in his bed. And many a successful person doesn't seem, even as you've just said, to have done anything to merit his success."

The Master: "That is true. The law of karma is therefore inextricable from its companion, the law of reincarnation. Each would be incomplete without the other.

"One lifetime is not enough to close the circle of countless acts that are initiated during a person's sojourn on earth."

6

"It seems unfair," a disciple lamented, "that we should be punished for mistakes that we made unintentionally, without realizing they were wrong."

"Ignorance," replied the Master, "doesn't alter the law. If a person drives his car absent-mindedly into a tree, his resulting injuries won't be fewer because he was absent-minded.

"You must learn to adapt your actions to the law. As Sri Yukteswarji remarked once to me, 'The cosmos would be fairly chaotic if its laws could not operate without the sanction of human belief.'"[5]

7

A disciple: "It all seems hopelessly complex, Master. Just think how many laws are passed in a single year by the government of one country. The laws of the universe, then, must number infinity!"

The Master, chuckling: "Really, it isn't quite so complicated as it seems. In the Bhagavad Gita, the forces of evil are described as many, while those on the side of good number only a few. Jesus Christ, too, described the way to perdition as a broad highway—but, he said, 'strait is the gate, and narrow is the way, which leadeth unto life.'[6]

"The ways of error are endlessly winding, but the way out of error is direct. A few simple rules will suffice. And the most important of these is simply this: Love God.

"To one who loves much, Jesus said, much is forgiven."[7]

1   "Be not deceived; God is not mocked: for whatsoever a man soweth, that shall he also reap." (Galatians 6:7)
2   Chapter 12, "Years in My Master's Hermitage."
3   Genesis 9:6.
4   John 5:14.
5   *Autobiography of a Yogi*, Chapter 16, "Outwitting the Stars."
6   Matthew 7:14.
7   Luke 7:47.

Chapter 9

THE LESSON OF REINCARNATION

1

Paramhansa Yogananda said: "Why is a baby born crippled? Only reincarnation can explain this fact satisfactorily. People behold it as a 'sweet, innocent' baby, but in some past life that personality must have transgressed against God's law. This transgression deprived him of the consciousness of having good legs. Thus—and because the mind controls the body—when that person came back again into a physical body he wasn't able to create a perfect pair of legs, and was born crippled.

"Why is one person born a moron and another, intelligent? God would be very unjust, wouldn't He, if He allowed such things to happen without a cause. But there *is* a cause. For what we are now is the result of our own actions at various times in the past.

"In our souls we are immortal, but in our personalities we cannot reclaim the consciousness of that immortality until our human imperfections have all been rubbed away. Working on ourselves is like chipping and polishing away the extraneous stone on a statue, until the image that was hidden is revealed in all its perfection."

2

A newcomer to the teachings: "Why must we reincarnate? If we all came from God, then, after death, why don't we simply merge back into Him?"

Paramhansa Yogananda: "If our individuality were dissolved by death we would do so indeed. But the ego forms the physical body. It is the cause, not the effect, of physical birth.

"The ego is an element of the astral body, which is retained after physical death. The physical body is merely the ego's projection into the material world.

"God cannot be attained by so simple an act as merely dying! To die is easy, but it is very difficult to attain that high level of consciousness in which the soul can merge back into Infinity.

"What, indeed, would worldly people do if they found themselves confronted with such a possibility? What would they do, for that matter, even in heaven? They would complain about everything, and go on arguing and fighting among themselves, just as they did on earth. And in the process, they'd only turn heaven itself into another kind of hell!

"After death, the basic tendencies of a person's nature remain just what they were on earth. Al Capone, the gangster, didn't suddenly become an angel by departing this plane of existence! Criminals retain their evil tendencies until they themselves work them out, perhaps after incarnations, and after many hard lessons: until their avarice, for example, has been transformed into a desire to help others; their lawlessness into a desire to uphold the law; and their cruelty into kindness to all."

Newcomer: "What causes the ego to reincarnate?"

Yogananda: "Desire. Desire, you see, directs energy. As long as a person desires the things of earth, he must come back here, where alone his desires can be fulfilled. If he longs for cigarettes, or motor cars, or money, the astral world can't provide those things. He will have to return to earth, where such things can be obtained."

A disciple: "Must every desire conceived on earth be fulfilled here also?"

Yogananda: "Not pure desires—not, for example, the longing for beautiful music, expansive scenery, or harmonious relationships. Such desires can be fulfilled better in the astral world than on this imperfect material plane.

"In many cases, the desire to create beauty here on earth is due to deeper-than-conscious memories of the beauty and harmony one experienced in the astral world."

--◦ 3 ◦--

A visitor: "How much does the soul experience of its life in the astral world? Does it remain there for many years after leaving the physical plane?"

The Master: "It depends on your degree of spiritual evolution. Materialistic souls—I use the word *soul* here in the sense you have, though in fact the soul is ever perfect; it is ego-consciousness that one carries with him into the astral world. Materialistic 'souls,' then, are so hypnotized by what they think of as matter's reality that they are not sensitive to subtler realms of existence. Such persons, after death, fall into a deep sleep. If at all they wake up later on, they may find themselves surrounded by darkness or by a kind of grey mist. They don't know where they are. If on earth they lived evil lives, they may suffer nightmares, and be tormented by demons.

"After some time, they are reborn in a new body to continue the long climb toward spiritual enlightenment.

"Those with more spiritual tendencies, on the other hand, develop, through their virtuous deeds and inclinations, a degree of intuition. They are therefore more sensitive to that other world after death, and are able more consciously to enjoy its beauty. Having raised their own vibrations by good deeds, they are attracted to higher vibrations in the astral realm.

"Those souls, especially, who in this life have meditated even a little bit, go to regions of great beauty after death.

"Those also go to higher regions who have prized duty and truth above their physical existence."

Visitor: "Do even soldiers, then, who die in battle go to heaven?"

The Master: "If they died for duty and truth."

Visitor: "What is heaven like?"

The Master: "There are two kinds of heaven. The one most people think of is that which comprises the higher regions of the astral world. The true heaven, however, and the one to which Jesus more often referred, is the state of union with God.

"The astral heaven has, as Jesus described it, many 'mansions,' or levels of vibration. It is similar to this material world, for this one is a projection of those subtler realms. The astral heaven, however, is without the countless imperfections of this grosser plane of existence.

"Heaven is not 'up there,' as people commonly imagine. It is all around us. It is just behind our physical vision. I see it all the time, and I spend much of my time there. It is a vast universe, composed of beautiful lights, sounds, and colors. The colors of the material plane are very dull by comparison. Heaven's beauty is like the most radiant sunset you have ever seen, and even far more beautiful.

"There is infinite variety in the astral world. The seasons there can be changed at will by advanced souls. Usually it is springtime there, with perennial sunshine. Snow, when it falls, is peaceful and beautiful, and not at all cold. When the rain falls, it descends gently, as myriad-colored lights.

"Sentiments, too, are highly refined on the astral plane, and far more intense than people normally experience them on earth.

"Heaven is not an idle place. Its inhabitants are very active. All the vibrations of this material universe are controlled by angels. Astral beings, though busy, are at the same time very happy.

"Sometimes, in their compassion for mankind, they visit people in dreams or in visions, or inspire in them beautiful thoughts.

"How long a person remains in the astral world depends on how well he lived on earth. Those with good karma may remain there for many centuries. Devotees, on the other hand, spurred on by their desire for enlightenment, may elect to return to earth sooner, in order to continue their spiritual efforts. For they realize that the astral world, too, is but a veil behind which the Lord hides His face of eternal perfection."

4

"Master," asked a disciple, "how are souls reborn on earth?"

"After passing some time in the astral world," Yogananda replied, "the length of their stay depending on their stored-up good karma, the material desires in their subconscious become reawakened. They are then drawn back to earth, or to some other planet in the material universe, by the magnetic attraction of desire.

"At the time of physical conception, there is a flash of light in the ether. Souls in the other world that await physical rebirth, when the vibrations of that light are compatible to their own, rush towards it. Sometimes more than one soul enters a womb at the same time. Thus, twins are born."

Disciple: "Are spiritual souls always born into spiritual families?"

The Master: "Like attracts like; that is the general rule. Many factors enter in, however—timing, for example, and availability. For saintly souls, opportunities for reincarnation into highly evolved families are not many, for spiritual people often prefer not to marry and have children. There is, moreover, the question of individual karma, with all its complexities.

"People are a mixture of many qualities. Sometimes it happens that a saint is born to criminal parents, if he shares with them a strong attraction, for instance, to peace.

"For couples desiring spiritual children," the Master continued, "it is important that they keep their consciousness uplifted when coming together in physical union. For their vibrations at that moment will determine the quality of the flash of light in the astral world.

"A couple once told me they wanted a spiritual child, and asked me to help them to attract such a soul to them. I showed them a photograph of a child who had died, and who, I felt intuitively, was karmically ready for rebirth. They felt drawn to the photograph. I then told them, 'Remain sexually abstinent for the next six months, and meditate daily. During meditation, concentrate on this photo, and invite this being into your home.' They did so. And at the end of that time the wife conceived. This was the very soul that was born to them."

⊷5⊷

A disciple: "Sir, if a white person is prejudiced against blacks, won't it follow that in his next life he himself will be born black?"

Paramhansa Yogananda laughed. "That's perfectly true! Aversion is just as strong a magnetic force as attraction.

"God is not impressed by human prejudices.

"Sometimes," he continued, "you see whole families who do nothing but fight amongst themselves. They were enemies before—attracted together into the same home, where now they must work out their hatred at close quarters!

"There is the story of a church in one of the southern states of America. It was a place where only white people were allowed to attend the services.

"Jim, the Negro janitor, wanted more than anything else to be permitted to worship with the congregation on Sunday mornings. 'Jim,' the minister explained to him, 'I'd love to have you join us. But if you did so, you know I'd lose my job.'

"One night Jim prayed broken-heartedly to Jesus, 'Lord, why can't I worship in there with the white folk?' After some time he fell asleep, and a vision was granted him: Jesus Christ appeared in a great light, smiling compassionately.

"'My son,' Jesus said, 'don't feel too badly. For twenty years I've been trying to enter that very church myself, and I haven't yet succeeded!'"

⇥ 6 ⇤

Two disciples, working together on a project for the Master, were surprised to find a sudden and apparently causeless animosity spring up between them. They soon overcame their feelings, and in time developed a sincere respect for each other. Later, one of them asked the Master, "Why did both of us feel such an instant aversion?"

"You were enemies in a former life," the Master explained.

"Our emotions," he remarked on another occasion, "do not represent us as we really are, in our souls. The soul is ever loving, and ever filled with joy. Emotions, however, cloud that eternal reality.

"To find freedom, we must calm the waves of emotion, and dwell ever calmly in the consciousness of love and joy."

⇢●7●⇠

"The lesson of reincarnation is to neutralize the waves of likes and dislikes, of desire and aversion, by the expression of kindness, forgiveness, and compassion to all, and by steadfast contentment in the Self. We must love others not for their human personalities, but because they are manifestations of God, Who dwells equally in all."

⇢●8●⇠

"If you ridicule or condemn others, then at some time, in this life or in some future life, you will have to undergo the same experiences as those of whom you now disapprove so uncharitably."

⇢●9●⇠

A disciple, after five months with Paramhansa Yogananda in the desert, said, "I have always wanted to go off and live alone like this."

"That," the Master replied, "is because you have done it before in former lives. Most of those who are with me have lived alone many times in the past."

⇢❧ 10 ❧⇠

A disciple: "Was I a yogi in past lives?"
Yogananda: "Many times. You would have to have been, to be living here."[1]

⇢❧ 11 ❧⇠

A disciple once lamented, "I don't think I have very good karma, Master."
Emphatically Paramhansa Yogananda replied, "Remember this: It takes very, *very*, VERY good karma for a person even to want to know God!"

⇢❧ 12 ❧⇠

A disciple: "Master, why can't I remember my past incarnations?"
"It is better so, usually," replied the Master with a humorous smile. "People would soon grow discouraged if they knew all the things they'd done wrong in the past! God gives them an opportunity to try again, without the false hypnosis that they *are* their mistakes.
"The less attached you are to the body," he continued, "especially during deep meditation, the more clearly you will remember your past lives and everything that you ever did in each one of them."

⇥ 13 ⇤

"It wouldn't help most people to remember their past. Even in this lifetime, see how habit-bound many of them become. I call them psychological antiques! Everything they do is predictable. Even the melodies they whistle or sing are the same—year in, and year out. And the older they grow, the more settled they become in all their ways of thinking, feeling, and behaving.

"Such people need the opportunity to forget what they've done and what they've been, and to start afresh. Only in a new beginning is there any hope of their making something better of themselves."

⇥ 14 ⇤

"As long as you enjoy living and acting in this dream of delusion, so long will you go on, for incarnation after incarnation, experiencing the pains and pleasures of this world and this body. The Bhagavad Gita describes it as a great wheel, endlessly turning.

"If, however, you desire strongly to get out you *must* be released.

"Remember, freedom is your eternal destiny."

---

1   i.e., as his disciple.

Chapter 10

Working Out Karma

-»⊛ 1 ⊛«-

"It all seems so complicated, Master," lamented a disciple. "I can see that karma and reincarnation belong together. But when I think of all the actions one initiates in a single lifetime, and then multiply them by God-knows-how-many-more lifetimes, I'm appalled. The interactions of cause and effect must be literally endless!"

"So they are," agreed the Master, "as long as one tries to work out his karma in the outer world. One desire leads to another, and that one to still others. Every desire must be fulfilled, every action brought to completion."

"Even trivial desires?" pursued the disciple in dismay. "What about some little wish that I might have had once, years ago, for an ice cream cone?"

"Even that," replied the Master emphatically. "Any energy that you put out, however slight, must return to you eventually."

The disciple flung his hands up in despair. "Then it all seems quite hopeless! As well might one try calming the waves on the ocean!"

"It is a big job, I grant you," Yogananda said. "Still, it isn't nearly so difficult as it looks. For, ask yourself this: What is it that causes the waves to rise and fall in the first place? It's the wind. Without wind, the surface grows calm automatically. Similarly, when the storm of delusion abates in the mind, the waves of action and reaction subside automatically.

"So what you must do is still the waves of your mind by deep meditation, and then, in meditation, rid yourself of the consciousness of ego-involvement. Once you cease seeing yourself as the causative agent, the waves of delusion may continue to rise and fall outwardly, but you yourself will no longer be affected by them."

"Would it be helpful," inquired the disciple, "to stop acting altogether?"

"Just try it!" The Master smiled. "You'll see that it simply isn't possible to stop acting. Even the decision not to act would be an outward projection of your ego; it would therefore constitute action of a kind.

"I once met a man in Phoenix, Arizona," he continued, "who was disheveled, his clothing a confusion of dirty rags. I said to him, 'Why do you dress like that? You aren't so poor that you need to.'

"'I'm a renunciate,' the man declared proudly.

"'On the contrary,' I told him, 'you are attached all over again, this time to disorder.'

"The Bhagavad Gita teaches that no one can escape action—karma, in other words—by refraining from action. But the Gita also teaches an invaluable method for escaping karma. What it recommends is *nishkam karma:* desireless action, that is, action without desire for the fruits of action. If you act thus, you will gradually attain freedom from the bondage of karma.

"During activity, never feel that it is you who are acting. Act, instead, with the thought that God is the Doer. Pray to Him, 'Lord, Thou art acting through me.'

"Even when you make mistakes, make Him responsible for them. He likes that! Of course, you mustn't deliberately do wrong and then lay the blame on Him! But if you do your best but still fail, give your failure to Him. Cling to the thought that you are ever free in your Self. This is the way to final freedom in the Lord.

"Of course, other things are involved, too: devotion, meditation, divine grace, and so on. But as far as action is concerned, desireless action is the pathway to freedom."

―◦― 2 ―◦―

"If I had no desires," asked a congregation member, "wouldn't I lose all motivation, and become a sort of automaton?"

"Many people imagine so," Yogananda replied. "They think they'd have no further interest in life. But that isn't what happens at all. Rather, you would find life to be infinitely more interesting.

"Consider the negative aspect of desire. It keeps you forever fearful. 'What if this happens?' you think; or, 'What if that doesn't happen?' You live in a state of anxiety for the future, or of regret for the past.

"Non-attachment, on the other hand, helps you to live perpetually in a state of inner freedom and happiness. When you can be happy in the present, then you have God.

"Desirelessness doesn't rob you of motivation. Far from it! The more you live in God, the deeper the joy you experience in serving Him."

―◦― 3 ―◦―

"Even when indulging a bad habit, because you can't help yourself, let your mind be constantly resistant to it. Never accept that bad habit as a definition of who you really are, within."

⊶4⊷

"One of the monks here was having a hard time struggling against temptation. I said to him one day, 'I don't ask that you overcome delusion. All I ask is that you *resist* it.'"

⊶5⊷

"Bad karmic tendencies can be overcome not by concentrating on them, but by developing their opposite good tendencies. Hence the importance of serving God. By service to Him, through others, you automatically divert toward the development of good tendencies that energy which wants to take you in wrong, self-serving directions.

"Be ever busy for God. When you are not meditating, be active for Him. And when meditating, offer your mind up to Him in the same spirit of service, with keen, alert attention. Keep the mind ever busy with God, and with doing good for others.

"An idle mind is the workshop of the devil."

⊶6⊷

"You must be intensely active for God, if you would attain that actionless state of final union with Him."

-»=7=«-

"Never let your mind be seduced by restlessness, through joking too much, too many distractions, and so on. Be deep. As soon as you succumb to restlessness, all the old troubles will begin to exert their pull on the mind once again: sex, wine, and money.

"Of course, a little fun and laughter is good, occasionally. But don't let light-mindedness possess you. I, too, like to laugh sometimes, as you know. But when I choose to be serious, nothing and no one can draw me out of my inner Self.

"Be deep in everything you do. Even when laughing, don't lose your inner calmness. Be joyful inside, but always inwardly a little withdrawn. Be centered in the joy within.

"Dwell always in the Self. Come down a little bit when you have to, to eat, or talk, or to do your work; then withdraw into the Self again.

"Be calmly active, and actively calm. That is the way of the yogi."

-»=8=«-

"Objective conditions are always neutral. It is how you react to them that makes them appear sad or happy.

"Work on yourself: on your reactions to outer circumstances. This is the essence of yoga: to neutralize the waves of reaction in the heart. Be ever happy inside. You will never be able to change things outwardly in such a way as to make them ever pleasing to you.

"Change yourself."

9

"A good rule in life is to tell yourself simply, 'What comes of itself, let it come.'"

10

"In India there has been much too much emphasis on karma. 'Karma! Karma!' they cry. 'It's my karma. I can do nothing about it!'

"Absurd! Karma is simply action. Whatever has been done can just as certainly be undone.

"Americans have, to a much greater extent than in India, the consciousness that everything is possible. 'If it can be done,' I've heard many people say here, 'we will do it. And if it is impossible, we will do it anyway. It may just take us a little longer.'

"'Eventually?' Americans say. 'Eventually? Why not *now*?' That is the spirit that I like so much in this country!"

11

To a struggling disciple: "Your job, for now, is to get to God. Don't worry about all the karma you will still have to complete. Let God worry about that!

"First, destroy in yourself the source of karmic involvement. That source is your attachment to the ego. Once the ego is merged in Him, then any actions you perform will no longer revert to yourself. Your actions will be like writing on water: They will leave no trace in the mind. In severing yourself from egoic involvement in any action that you perform, you will have cut the Gordian knot of delusion.

"This is the state of the *jivan mukta*, one who is free inside even while living in this world. Being inwardly free, nothing he does can ever affect him again."

⊷ 12 ⊶

"First, by deep meditation and by living for God alone, calm the waves of thought and desire that constitute your present reality. Once you attain deep calmness within, you will be able to work on calming the waves that lie at a greater distance from this reality.

"In superconsciousness you will behold everything clearly at last as it truly is. The *jivan mukta*, through visions, may work out the karma of an entire lifetime in one meditation. If he reincarnates, he may even do so simultaneously in several bodies, in order the more quickly to work out his past karma.

"Once all his past karma has been worked out, he becomes a *siddha*, or *param mukta:* a perfected being. If ever such a freed soul reincarnates, he does so purely for the welfare of humanity, and not from any karmic need of his own. Such a one is an *avatar*, or descended master: an incarnation of God.

"The important thing, first, is to get to God. Once you succeed in bringing His light into the dimly lit room of your consciousness, your spiritual darkness will vanish forever."

⇥ 13 ⇤

"Always, in all things, behold God as the Doer.

"It is a matter of inner attitude. It isn't the outward show of humility that so many devotees assume from a desire to impress others.

"A little story will illustrate what I mean.

"The gopis[1] used to go every day to bring fresh cheese to Krishna. One day, the river Jamuna was in spate, and the gopis couldn't cross it to reach him. 'What shall we do?' they cried.

"And then they remembered Byasa, a great devotee of Krishna, who lived on their own side of the river.

"'Byasa is a saint,' they cried. 'Let us go to him. Perhaps he'll perform a miracle for us and help us somehow to get across the river.' They went and asked him to help them reach Krishna.

"'Krishna! Krishna!' Byasa shouted, pretending to be displeased. 'All I ever hear is Krishna! What about *me*?'

"Well, the gopis were very embarrassed! The cheese was for Krishna, but still, they didn't dare refuse Byasa a taste of it since they'd asked him to help them. So they offered him a little bit. And Byasa ate, and ate, and ate, apparently with the greatest relish.

"When he'd eaten as much as his stomach could hold, he somehow carried himself to the river bank, and there he cried, 'O river Jamuna, if I have not eaten anything, divide up and part!'

"'What a liar!' the gopis whispered among themselves. 'Just see how he has gorged himself. And now he dares to command the river's obedience on the very condition that he hasn't eaten a thing!'

"At that moment the river parted! Not pausing to ponder this mystery, the gopis rushed across to the other side. There, as they approached Krishna's hut, they found him asleep.

"'What's this?' they wondered. Usually Krishna was standing outside his hut, eagerly awaiting their visit—and the cheese.

"'Lord,' they cried, 'aren't you hungry today?'

"'Hm?' replied Krishna, opening his eyes sleepily.

"'We've brought you your cheese, Lord.'

"'Oh, thank you,' said Krishna. 'But I'm no longer hungry.'

"'But why? Has someone fed you already?'

"'Oh, yes,' he replied. 'That fellow, Byasa, on the other bank has fed me too much already.'

"Byasa, you see, had offered the food first to Krishna, and had thought of him constantly while eating it. He didn't eat in ego-consciousness, but only in the thought that Krishna was eating through him.

"In that way, every devotee should feel that God is acting through him.

"Stop dwelling on the thought of 'I, I'! Sing ever in your heart, instead, 'Thou, Thou, Lord, only Thou!'"

14

"Go to God, and all the problems that lie buried within the soil of your consciousness will be swept away in a single stroke.

"The caverns of many lives lie buried in your mental soil. All the desires you've ever had in the past are stored in them, waiting to attract you to material things. But if you go back to God, you will be able to satisfy all those desires forever in His bliss."

⇥ 15 ⇤

"Sir," inquired a disciple, "if the thing that keeps us bound to this world is our desire for it, why aren't those people liberated who commit suicide? Surely they, at least, have no desire to remain here. Just look at the extreme measures they employ to get away!"

The Master chuckled at this absurdity as he replied, "But there must also be a positive desire for God!"

On other occasions he said, of suicide, "Life is a school from which you must graduate into Infinite Consciousness. If you play truant, you will only have to return here again and again, as many times as it takes you to learn life's supreme lesson."

⇥ 16 ⇤

"In working out karma, so long as you are still afraid of it you won't yet be completely free.

"Karma is best worked out by meeting pleasantly every test that comes, and by accepting courageously any hardship that your tests impose."

⇥ 17 ⇤

"An important factor in overcoming karma is meditation. Every time you meditate, your karma decreases, for at that time your energy is focused in the brain and burns up the old brain cells.

"After every deep meditation, you will find yourself becoming freer inside."

⇥18↤

"Karma is greatly mitigated by the help of the guru. The guru sees your karma, and knows what you need to do, to get out of it.

"He also assumes much of your karmic burden, even as a strong man might help a weaker by carrying some of his load. Again, if the weaker man is about to be struck a severe blow, the stronger may be able to step in the way and take it upon himself.

"Such is the priceless value of the guru's help. Without a guru, the spiritual path is like trying to walk in quicksand when there is a paved highway nearby, going in the same direction."

⇥19↤

"The spiritual path is twenty-five percent the disciple's effort, twenty-five percent the guru's effort on his behalf, and fifty percent the grace of God.

"Don't forget, however," the Master warned, "that the twenty-five percent that is your part represents one hundred percent of your own effort and sincerity!"

⤞20⤝

"The desires of incarnations keep one endlessly wandering. Once, however, a sincere longing for God awakens in the heart, liberation is already assured, even though the process take more incarnations. For that longing for God, too, is a desire, and must be fulfilled eventually."

⤞21⤝

The seven-year-old child of a disciple of the Master lost his finger in an accident. The following day, the boy declared staunchly, "It would have been much worse without Master's blessings." These words were reported to Yogananda, who repeated them later to a few of the monks, evidently because he endorsed them.

"The day before the accident," the Master continued, "I saw a black cloud above him. I knew then that some karmic misfortune was about to befall him."

It is an interesting fact that Paramhansa Yogananda's disciples always received protection, often in miraculous ways.[2]

A feature of the way karma works may be seen in the fact of that black cloud. From other things that the Master said and wrote, it is clear that if a person's aura[3] is strong, the negative consequences of his bad karma will have a greatly lessened impact on him, even though the karma must, of necessity, return to him. For, as the Bible puts it, "It must needs be that offenses come."[4]

A strong aura might be compared to the protection an umbrella gives when it rains. Thus, the Master frequently counseled the wearing of astrological bangles as a means of artificially strengthening the aura. As he explained in the chapter, "Outwitting the Stars," from *Autobiography of a Yogi*, quoting his guru Sri Yukteswar, certain pure metals, and especially faultless gems of not less than two carats, emit an astral light that is powerfully counteractive to negative influences.

To this counsel, however, Paramhansa Yogananda would often add, "Never forget that devotion to God is the greatest 'bangle.'"

⟶◉ 22 ◉⟵

"When traveling on the ocean, one comes upon areas, here or there, where the sea is calm. Even so, on the great ocean of delusion one finds, occasionally, areas of exceptional calmness. This happens when an *avatar*, or divine incarnation, is sent to earth with a special dispensation. All who come to him and tune in to his spirit find it relatively easy to escape delusion's power."

⟶◉ 23 ◉⟵

At a Kriya initiation in December, 1948, Paramhansa Yogananda said: "Of those present, there will be a few *siddhas*,[5] and quite a few *jivan muktas*."[6]

⟶◉ 24 ◉⟵

"Those who are with me[7] I never have any trouble with. Just a glance with the eyes is enough. It is much better when I can talk with the eyes. Most of them are saints from former lives."

1   Girl cowherds, and devotees of Krishna during his legendary boyhood in Gokul.

2   See *The Path*, Chapter 23, "God Protects His Devotees," by Kriyananda, Crystal Clarity Publishers, Nevada City, California.

3   The astral light surrounding the body.

4   Matthew 18:7.

5   Explained on page 105 (#12).

6   Explained on page 104-5 (#11).

7   i.e., "Those who are in tune with me."

Chapter 11

GRACE VS. SELF-EFFORT

25

"Sir," asked a disciple, "is it possible for a soul to be lost forever?"

"Impossible!" the Master replied. "The soul is a part of God. How would it be possible to destroy God?"

26

"St. Anthony spent years meditating in a tomb in the desert. All the while he was tormented by devils. At last Satan threatened to destroy him if he wouldn't give up his search for God. The walls of the tomb started to crack. They threatened to fall in upon him, crushing him. The friezes of animals on the walls of the tomb assumed living form and converged upon him to devour him.

"Anthony looked up once more in prayer, and called out to Christ.

"Suddenly a great light appeared. Jesus Christ stood there at last, gazing calmly down. In an instant, the darkness of Satan vanished. In the ecstasy of divine awakening, St. Anthony recalled all those incarnations that he had been seeking God.

"Oh!" the Master cried, "I know that experience. What joy comes with it!

"And Anthony cried out from the very depths of his soul, 'Lord! Where were you all those years that I cried for you to come?'

"And the Lord, with a loving smile, replied, 'Anthony, I was with you always.'"

→ 1 ←

"Every religious group I've encountered in this country tells its members they don't have to work for their
salvation—'lest any man should boast,' they explain, quoting
St. Paul.[1] Their doctrine of salvation is based entirely on
belief: Believe as they do, and you'll be saved by God's grace.
Many make church membership a further condition for salvation, the implication being that, if anything more needs doing,
the church will do it for you.

"However, didn't Jesus tell his followers, 'Why call ye me
Lord, Lord, and do not the things which I say?'[2]

"Suppose you want riches. Will you sit in a room and wait
for God to give them to you simply because you believe in
Him? Hardly! You'll work very hard to earn them. Why,
then, expect salvation to come to you effortlessly, just because
you believe?

"And what of that further condition for salvation: joining
the right church? Salvation is a personal matter between each
soul and God. You have to individually make love to God.
Church membership may be helpful, if it fosters an inward
relationship with Him, but outward membership is no guarantee of this inward relationship, and it is certainly no substitute for it.

"If anybody tells you that church membership will give you
God, ask him if his church can eat for you vicariously as well.
If it can't fill your body without effort on your own part to
eat the food, why should you accept that it will fill your soul
without spiritual effort on your part?

"Salvation means freedom from ego-limitation, which is
imposed on the soul through attachment to body-consciousness. Salvation can come only by great personal effort.

"It is true that others can *help* you in your effort. It is
true also that God's grace alone can save you; St. Paul was

perfectly correct in what he said. Nevertheless, your sincere effort must be there also. Without great effort on your part, you will never attain salvation."

-- 2 --

"Master," said a disciple, "J—— is a little discouraged. Someone told him that, according to Ramakrishna,[3] grace is only a sport of God. He takes this to mean that one might meditate for years and get nowhere, yet God might reveal Himself to any drunkard if He took a mere notion to do so."

The Master replied, "Ramakrishna would never have said that! That is what happens when people without spiritual realization try to interpret the sayings of the masters. God is not a creature of whims! Of course, it may *look* like sport sometimes to people who don't see the causal influences of past karma. But why would God go against His own law? He Himself created the law."

-- 3 --

"There is so much confusion in religion on the subject of grace. People think God wants to be pleased, personally, as His condition for answering their prayers. They cast God in their own image, instead of going deep within in meditation to discover how it is that they are made in His image.

"God doesn't need propitiating! His grace isn't based on personal likes and dislikes. It is true that He responds to the devotee's love, but that love, too, must be impersonal. It must be free of ego-motivation."

---⊷4⊷---

"What is grace? People confuse it with divine favor, as though God could be bought, or cajoled into doing something that He would not do otherwise.

"I knew a man who once put a hundred dollars in the collection plate during a church service on Sunday morning. Later on, he expressed disappointment that God hadn't answered the prayer that accompanied his offering. Well, God already *was* that offering! God watches the heart, not the collection plate!

"It is almost as bad when people say that, to be saved, you must 'Believe! Believe! Believe!' Do they think God needs reassurance, through their belief in Him? He watches what they are inside, not their opinions about things.

"A person who considers himself an atheist may sometimes, in fact, be closer to God, because of his love for other people, than many who believe in God with their minds, but whose actions towards their fellowman are uncharitable. God, again, watches people's deeds, not their words.

"Of course, it is always good to give money to a spiritual cause. One creates good karma by doing so. It is also better to believe in God than to deny Him, for without belief you won't make the effort to find Him. But don't imagine that God can be bribed or flattered into giving you His grace. The only thing that can win Him is your love.

"What, then, is grace? It is God's power, as distinct from any lesser power. Because God is the only Reality, His also is the only power in existence. Seen in this light, our merely human efforts are illusory. It is His power, even when we draw on it unconsciously, that accomplishes everything that we achieve in life. And our failures are due to lack of attunement on our part with that power.

"God's grace flows into us, the more we open ourselves to Him. It doesn't come to us from outside. It is the operation, from within, of our own higher reality. Grace comes, the more we live in soul-consciousness, and the less we live centered in the ego."

⊷5⊷

"In the history of religion there is a perennial debate as to which is more important: divine grace (*kripa*, as it is called in India), or human effort. The answer is quite simple, and the masters have tried repeatedly to convey it to people in their teachings.

"Man must do his best, of course. His best, however, will be crowned with success to the extent that he realizes that it isn't he, as a human being, who is acting, but God who is acting through him, inspiring and guiding him.

"To think of God as the Doer doesn't make a person passive. It takes a great effort of will to be receptive to Him. The devotee must offer himself positively and joyfully into the flow of inner grace.

"The power that is in you is *your own, but God-given.* Use it; God won't use it for you. The more you attune your will, during activity, to His infinite will, the more you will find His power and blessing strengthening and guiding you in everything you do."

⊷6⊷

"Pray this way to God: 'Lord, I will reason, I will will, I will act, but guide Thou my reason, will, and activity to the right course in everything.'"

→►◎ 7 ◎◄←

"God doesn't always answer your prayers in the way that you expect, but, if your faith in Him never wavers, He will grant you far *more* than you expect."

→►◎ 8 ◎◄←

A disciple: "What is the difference, Master, between faith and belief?"

Yogananda: "Belief is mental. It is like the hypotheses of science, which require testing by experimentation. Belief, in other words, is provisional. Its premises must be tested in the 'laboratory' of meditation, and proved in the direct experience of God.

"Test your beliefs—not in a doubting spirit. Test them because you want to *know* the truth, and not merely to think about it.

"'Faith,' St. Paul said, 'is the proof of things unseen.'[4] It isn't that belief itself proves the existence of higher realities, any more than people's belief that the world was flat made it so. The actual experience of higher realities, however, gives one faith in them. That is what St. Paul meant. With inner verification alone comes faith.

"There is much in your life that might give you faith even now. You don't have to wait for visions to give it to you. Go by what you've experienced already. Don't keep your religion on a merely mental level.

"Have you ever felt God's peace in meditation? Have you felt His love touching your heart? Aren't these already something real and meaningful to you? Cling to them. Make experience the basis of your faith. As Jesus said, 'We speak that which we *know*.'⁵ Build on what you already know. As Jesus said also, 'Whosoever hath, to him shall be given, and he shall have more abundance.'⁶

"Swami Shankaracharya, a great master in ancient India, was on the opposite bank of a river from where a close disciple of his was standing. With a quiet smile he called to his disciple, 'Come here!'

"Unhesitatingly, the young man stepped onto the water. And behold, a lotus leaf rose up and supported his foot! With every step another leaf appeared until he had crossed the river, where he cast himself at the Master's feet. From that day onwards he became known as *Padmapada*, 'Lotus Feet.'

"Padmapada had had no experience of his guru's power to create lotus leaves to support people's feet. He *had*, however, experienced his guru's power in other ways. He therefore drew on that experience, instead of blocking it out of his life with rational doubts and mental reservations."

9

"Faith means expanding your intuitive awareness of God's presence within, and not relying on reason as your chief means of understanding."

10

"Two ladies that I knew had a habit of leaving their car unlocked when they parked it. I once said to them, 'You should take the precaution of locking your car.'

"'What's the matter with you?' they cried. 'Where is your faith in God?'

"'I have faith,' I answered, 'but this is not faith you are exercising. It is carelessness. Why *should* God protect you, when you won't do anything to protect yourselves?'

"'Oh, the Lord watches over us,' they assured me. 'Nothing will be stolen.' So they kept on leaving their car as if half locked, but half open.

"Well, one day they had several thousand dollars' worth of bonds and other rare possessions in their car. They went off, leaving everything in the charge of their vaunted 'faith.' During their absence, thieves came and stole everything, with the exception of a minor item they'd somehow overlooked. One of the ladies lost all the money she'd been saving for years.

"Later I said to them, 'Why expect God to protect you if you ignore His laws of reason and common sense? Have faith, but at the same time be practical. Don't make unnecessary demands of God, nor expect Him to do everything for you just because you believe in Him. He *will* take care of you, but you must also do your share.'"

11

A woman disciple often took foolish risks, countering criticism with the argument, "If anything goes wrong, Master will protect me." One day this assertion was reported to Paramhansa Yogananda.

"Of all things!" he exclaimed. "Let her drive her car off a cliff and see whether I, or the Lord Himself, will protect her from the consequences of her folly! We must use our common sense, and not be outrageous in the demands we make of God.

"In the divine kingdom," he added, "there is no room for presumption."

⇥12⇤

"Faith must be cultivated. It cannot be achieved by mere wishful thinking. If you throw yourself off a mountaintop with the affirmation, 'God will protect me,' just see if He does! He expects you to use the common sense He has given you.

"He *will* take care of you, surely, if you do your best always, act sensibly, and leave the results in His hands. Faith, however, must be watered by inner experience, like a plant. The more you actually experience the care He takes of you, the more you will come to rely on Him—not fanatically, but naturally, in the divine way."

⇥13⇤

"The degree of faith, and of the flow of divine grace in your life, is determined by your depth of Self-realization. What you attempt to accomplish by grace should be tempered by what you have received of God's power in your life. Great miracles of faith, such as raising the dead to life, are possible only for those who have realized God as the sole Reality. For such miracles, mental affirmation, even if made very forcefully, is not enough.

"There was a man who had read in the Bible that faith can move mountains. The scriptural precept impressed him, particularly since, outside his bedroom window, there stood a hill that obstructed his view of a beautiful lake.

"One evening he decided to put the scripture to the test. Filled with unseasoned 'faith,' he prayed long and earnestly to the Father to remove that hill and cast it into the sea. As he went to bed, he looked forward anxiously to seeing the results of his prayer.

"Awaking the next morning, he rushed to the window and looked out. The hill hadn't budged an inch.

"'I *knew* you'd still be there!' he exclaimed.

"Such is faith, when it is mere affirmation."

—14—

"There are many stones lying about on the ground, but very few of them are diamonds. Spiritual truths, similarly, are not easy to find amid the confusion of human opinions.

"Divine grace is like the most precious of those rare diamonds. It is there to be found by all who will seek it diligently, but in order to find it one must do more than glance through a few books, or attend a few lectures. Grace cannot be found where people merely believe it to be. It must be sought in the right way, in the right place, and in the right spirit.

"The right spirit is an attitude of unconditional love for God. The right place is within yourself. The right way is in the silence of deep meditation.

"To find God, you must attune yourself to His ways."

1 "For by grace are ye saved through faith; and that not of yourselves: it is the gift of God: Not of works, lest any man should boast." (Ephesians 2:8,9)
2 Luke 6:46.
3 A great master of recent times in India.
4 "Now faith is the substance of things hoped for, the evidence of things not seen." (Hebrews 11:1) Paramhansa Yogananda read into this passage a deeper meaning than that usually ascribed to it, and changed the words slightly to correspond to his deeper insight.—*ed.*
5 John 3:11.
6 Matthew 13:12.

Chapter 12

THE NEED FOR YOGA

-»⊛ 1 ⊛«-

A visitor: "What is yoga?"

Paramhansa Yogananda: "Yoga means *union*. Etymologically, it is connected to the English word, *yoke*. Yoga means union with God, or, union of the little, ego-self with the divine Self, the infinite Spirit.

"Most people in the West, and also many in India, confuse yoga with Hatha Yoga, the system of bodily postures. But yoga is primarily a spiritual discipline.

"I don't mean to belittle the yoga postures. Hatha Yoga is a wonderful system. The body, moreover, is a part of our human nature, and must be kept fit lest it obstruct our spiritual efforts. Devotees, however, who are bent on finding God give less importance to the yoga postures. Nor is it strictly necessary that they practice them.

"Hatha Yoga is the physical branch of Raja Yoga, the true science of yoga. Raja Yoga is a system of meditation techniques that help to harmonize human consciousness with the divine consciousness.

"Yoga is an art as well as a science. It is a science, because it offers practical methods for controlling body and mind, thereby making deep meditation possible. And it is an art, for unless it is practiced intuitively and sensitively it will yield only superficial results.

"Yoga is not a system of beliefs. It takes into account the influence on each other of body and mind, and brings them into mutual harmony. So often, for instance, the mind cannot concentrate simply because of tension or illness in the body, which prevent the energy from flowing to the brain. So often, too, the energy in the body is weakened because the will is dispirited, or paralyzed by harmful emotions.

"Yoga works primarily with the energy in the body, through the science of *pranayama*, or energy-control. *Prana* means also 'breath.' Yoga teaches how, through breath-control, to still the mind and attain higher states of awareness.

"The higher teachings of yoga take one beyond techniques, and show the yogi, or yoga practitioner, how to direct his concentration in such a way as not only to harmonize human with divine consciousness, but to merge his consciousness in the Infinite.

"Yoga is a very ancient science; it is thousands of years old. The perceptions derived from its practice form the backbone of the greatness of India, which for centuries has been legendary. The truths espoused in the yoga teachings, however, are not limited to India, nor to those who consciously practice yoga techniques. Many saints of other religions also, including many Christian saints, have discovered aspects of the spiritual path that are intrinsic to the teachings of yoga.

"A number of them were what Indians, too, would accept as great yogis.

"They had raised their energy from body-attachment to soul-identity.

"They had discovered the secret of directing the heart's feeling upward in devotion to the brain, instead of letting it spill outward in restless emotions.

"They had discovered the portal of divine vision at the point between the eyebrows, through which the soul passes to merge in Christ consciousness.

"They had discovered the secrets of breathlessness, and how in breathlessness the soul can soar to the spiritual heights.

"They had discovered the state which some of them called mystical marriage, where the soul merges with God and becomes one with Him.

"Yoga completes the biblical teaching on how one should love God: with heart, mind, soul—*and strength*. For strength means energy.

"The ordinary person's energy is locked in his body. The lack of availability of that energy to his will prevents him from loving the Lord one-pointedly with any of the three other aspects of his nature: heart, mind, or soul. Only when the energy can be withdrawn from the body and directed upward in deep meditation is true inner communion possible."

-⦿ 2 ⦿-

"With a strong lens the sun's rays, focused through it, can ignite wood. Yoga practice, similarly, so concentrates the mind that the curtain of doubt and uncertainty is burned away, and the light of inner truth becomes manifest."

-⦿ 3 ⦿-

An adherent of another spiritual teaching objected that yoga practice would distract her from the exercise of devotion. "I want to be mad with love for God!" she cried. "The practice of techniques for finding Him is offensive to me. It seems so mechanical."

"So it can be, certainly," agreed the Master. "But it would be a mistake to practice yoga mechanically.

"A danger on the path of devotion is emotionalism. If one keeps blowing on a candle, how will it burn steadily? Similarly, if you keep stirring up your heart's feelings, you may become intoxicated emotionally, but how will you experience the deeper 'intoxication' of divine bliss?

"The Lord comes not in outward noise, nor when the mind is agitated, but in inner silence. His very being is silence. In silence He speaks to the soul.

"I do not mean it isn't good to cry for God, to shed tears of love for Him. But intense feeling, if expressed too much outwardly, soon exhausts itself.

"After singing to the Beloved and crying for Him to come, it is important that you rein in those awakened feelings, and channel them upward in the calmness of deep inner communion.

"The feelings experienced when the heart is restless are like a storm in a thimble compared to the oceanic love that bursts upon the soul when the heart is calm. If you grasp the bud of devotion too tightly, it won't be able to open its petals and spread them to receive the sun-rays of God's love. Only when you relax your heart's feelings can you channel them upward. And only then will they expand to embrace Infinity.

"Reflect: When talking to someone, isn't it normal to want also to hear his response? After praying and singing to God, then, why not listen for His answer in your soul? Meditation is that process of listening. Meditation is making yourself receptive to His silent inspirations within.

"The essence of yoga is the silence and receptivity that the practice of the techniques induces in the mind.

"So, be mad for God, yes, but more and more let that madness itself come from Him! Be intoxicated not with your own feelings, but with His rapture in your soul."

❧ 4 ❧

"Love for God should not be an outward show. To display to others your deep love for Him is a desecration of that most sacred of all relationships. Your love must be directed inward.

"This is why yoga practice is so important. It helps to direct one's feelings along the inner path which leads to Him.

"There was a famous woman saint in India named Mira. She was a *bhakta*, or devotee, who spent all her time singing to God. Mira was a saint, truly. But her husband was spiritually greater than she. She didn't even realize that he was spiritual, for he never spoke of God. And so it happened that, all the while he was in deep inner communion with the Lord, Mira kept praying for his conversion! It seemed to her that this was the only thing lacking in her life.

"One night, as they lay in bed together, she heard him cry to God in his sleep, 'My Infinite Beloved! Oh, when will You come and relieve the pangs of longing in my heart?'

"The following morning Mira addressed him joyfully, 'I've found you out!'

"'Don't say it!' he begged her earnestly.

"'Oh, you can't fool me any more! I realize now what a great devotee you are.'

"'I am so sorry you said that,' he replied. 'For now I must leave you. Long ago I made a promise to God that if anyone ever learned of my love for Him, I would leave this world.' He sat on the floor forthwith in the lotus pose, and left his body."

-»⊛ 5 ⊛«-

A student: "Why is concentration necessary?"

Yogananda: "Concentration is the key to success in everything. Even the businessman must be able to concentrate, or he won't achieve success in his worldly affairs.

"If you are talking with someone, and his eyes wander about the room and he keeps on fidgeting restlessly, won't you feel that he isn't really listening to you? After some time you may lose interest in further conversation with him.

"Don't expect, then, to win God's response until you can sit still and hold your mind open and attentive to His presence within."

-»⊛ 6 ⊛«-

A newcomer to the Self-Realization Fellowship church in Hollywood asked Paramhansa Yogananda, "Why are techniques necessary for developing concentration? Can't a person simply flow with the inspiration he feels when he prays?"

"A violinist may feel inspiration," Yogananda replied, "but if he doesn't learn techniques that have been developed through the experience of great musicians, he will never become more than an inspired amateur. Yoga techniques, in the same way, are necessary to help you to plumb the inner silence."

‒►◉ 7 ◉◄‒

"Master," lamented a disciple, "I have such difficulty in concentrating! I am faithful to my practice of the yoga techniques, but I never seem to get anywhere with them."

"Mechanical practice is not enough," the Master replied. "There must also be sincere interest in what you are doing. You must deepen your devotion.

"Just observe people at the movies. Don't they become yogis? See how still they sit during the suspenseful parts; how engrossed they are in the plot as it unfolds. All that absorption, simply because their interest has been aroused!

"Meditate in that way.

"Once you've convinced your mind that you really want to meet God in the inner silence, it will be easy for you to sit still and to meditate deeply."

‒►◉ 8 ◉◄‒

To the disciples, Yogananda often said, "Be patient in your yoga practice. A plant won't grow the moment you plant the seed. 'Make haste slowly,' as the saying goes. It may take time to achieve the results you long for, but the more you practice, the more you will see your life changing.

"The day will dawn at last when you won't even recognize yourself as the person you were."

⟶⟩◉ 9 ◉⟨⟵

"What happens," someone asked, "to those who try to reach God without the benefit of yoga techniques?"

"A few of them are successful," the Master replied, "if they came into this life with strong spiritual karma from the past. The great majority, however, even if they start out on the path with enthusiasm, gradually become discouraged.

"'Where is that God,' they ask finally, 'to Whom I've been praying all these years?' They attain a little inner peace, but over the years their prayers become increasingly a matter of habit, less one of inspiration.

"Rarely, in the West, have the centuries seen such great saints as there have been in India."

Chapter 13

THE HIGHWAY TO THE INFINITE

— 1 —

"What is the best religion?" queried a truth seeker.

"Self-realization," Yogananda replied.

"Self-realization is, in fact, the *only* religion. For it is the true purpose of religion, no matter how people define their beliefs. A person may be Christian or Jewish, Buddhist or Hindu, Muslim or Zoroastrian; he may proclaim that Jesus Christ is the only way, or Buddha, or Mohammed—as indeed, millions of believers do. He may insist that this ritual, or that place of worship, bestows salvation. But it all comes down to what he is, in himself.

"A thousand Christs wouldn't be able to give you God, if you didn't first make love to Him yourself.

"What does God care how you define Him? Could any dogma encompass Him, Who is everything and far more than everything? And don't you suppose that a Muslim or a Hindu who loves God is as dear to Jesus Christ as any Christian— and much more acceptable to him than those among his own followers who believe in God with their minds, but have no love for Him in their hearts?

"Jesus Christ didn't come to earth, nor does any great master come, to draw people to himself. He came to draw them to the truth—that truth which, Jesus said, 'shall make you free.'[1] The divine message is ever impersonal as it relates to this truth.

"At the same time, it is personal in its relation to the individual seeker. That is to say, the masters don't tell people, 'You will be saved by the religion you follow, outwardly.' They tell them, 'You will be saved by what you do, personally, to establish your kinship with God.'

"Self-realization is the eternal message of religion. Whatever your beliefs and practices, the essential purpose of religion is to help you to fulfill your own highest potential, as a child of God.

"The wave must realize that its reality, as a mere wave, is temporary. It may appear again and again as other waves, but in the end it *has* to realize that its reality lies not in its separateness as a wave, but in the ocean of which the wave is a manifestation. Realization of its true identity demands merging into the ocean and becoming one with it.

"Let us say a Jew becomes converted to Christianity. He stops going to the synagogue and goes, instead, to church. Does the simple fact of his conversion ensure his salvation? Not if it doesn't inspire him at the same time to love God more deeply.

"Your religion is not the garb you wear outwardly, but the garment of light you weave around your heart. By outward garb I don't mean your physical raiment only, but rather the thoughts and beliefs in which you enclose yourself. They are not *you*. Discover who you are, behind those outer trappings, and you will discover who Jesus was, and Buddha, and Krishna. For the masters come to earth for the purpose of holding up to every man a reflection of his deeper, eternal Self."

2

"My guru, Sri Yukteswar, liked a chant that I have translated, two lines from which go, '*Pranayama* be thy religion. *Pranayama* will give thee salvation.'

"*Pranayama* means control of the energy in the body, and its direction upward through the spine to the brain and to the Christ center between the eyebrows. This alone is the pathway of awakening. It isn't a matter of dogma or belief. It is simply the way we were all made by God.

"The consciousness enters the body by way of the brain and the spine. When the sperm and ovum unite to create the physical body, they do so at what becomes the medulla oblongata, at the base of the brain.

"From this medulla, the life-force moves out into the brain, down the spine and into the nervous system, then on to the muscles, etc., creating the body.

"The way out of the body, then, is to reverse this process. The difficulty in doing so lies in the fact that the life-force is already conditioned by birth to continue its outward direction—through the senses and onward to the environment as it is perceived through the senses. Thus, we think to possess the world and to enjoy it through the body.

"We can never experience anything outside ourselves, however, except vicariously, as the senses report their impressions to the brain. We may try to expand our understanding of the world by study, or our enjoyment of it through sense pleasures. The fact remains, we can never know anything except through the medium of the senses, so long as the life-force remains trapped in the body.

"There *is* a way out, however. It is for the life-force to merge with the cosmic energy; for the consciousness to merge in the infinite consciousness.

"The way to accomplish this end is to withdraw the life-force from the senses, and center it in the spine; to direct it upward through the spine to the brain, and thence out through the Christ center between the eyebrows.

"The ego is centered in the medulla oblongata. This is the negative pole of self-consciousness. The positive pole is situated at the Christ center. Concentration at this center—in the spiritual eye, the seat of spiritual vision—projects the consciousness beyond the ego into Infinity.

"The spine is the highway to the Infinite. Your own body is the temple of God. It is within your own self that God must be realized. Whatever places of pilgrimage you visit outwardly, and whatever outward rituals you perform, the ultimate 'pilgrimage' must be within. And the ultimate religious rite must be the offering of your life-force on the altar of inner God-communion.

"That was why Jesus said, 'Destroy this temple, and in three days I will raise it up.' 'He spake,' the Bible adds, 'of the temple of his body.'[2]

"This is the path of Kriya Yoga."[3]

—3—

"Does your teaching help people to be at peace with themselves?" inquired a visitor, a psychiatrist.

"Yes," replied the Master. "But that is the least that we teach. Our chief aim is to help people to be at peace with the Creator—to attain the perfection of peace in infinite consciousness."

—4—

"I once met a man in India who had been following the path of devotion for twenty years. I could see that, because of his devotion and sincerity, he was ready for an experience of God. But his devotional path had not given him that experience. He needed Kriya Yoga. He wouldn't accept it from me, however. He insisted on being loyal, as he thought, to his own path to God.

"'It isn't a question,' I explained, 'of changing your path to God. Kriya Yoga will guide you toward fulfillment in your path of devotion. But you are like a man who has lived for twenty years in a room, trying to get out through the walls, the ceiling, the floor. What I am offering to do, simply, is show you where the door is.'

"Well, finally he relented and took Kriya initiation. Within a week he had the experience of God that he'd been seeking those twenty years.

"Kriya Yoga," the Master concluded, "takes you onto the universal highway, where all by-paths of spiritual practice meet."

⇥ 5 ⇤

"I can take a few young men of the most restless sort, and let them practice Kriya for two hours every day in the way I tell them, and, without question, in four or five years I can make saints out of them.

"I won't preach a single sermon to them. I will simply tell them to practice Kriya for two hours a day, and they will see the difference in their lives. That is a good challenge.

"Of course, they must practice in the way that I tell them. That won't be easy. But it is surely worth the effort."

1 John 8:32.
2 John 2:19,21.
3 The technique most frequently referred to in *Autobiography of a Yogi*, and in my account of my life with Paramhansa Yogananda, The Path. Kriya Yoga is the highest technique on the path of Raja Yoga. —*ed.*

Chapter 14

THE NEED FOR A GURU

⇥ 1 ⇤

"The term, Self-realization," declared a rather imperi-
ous lady visitor, "appears to me to be totally incompatible
with the Hindu belief concerning the need for a guru. I find
Self-realization, as a concept, definitely attractive, but as
a Westerner, I'm afraid I am put off by this 'guru' concept.

"I believe in standing on one's own two feet, in taking one's
own hard knocks in life and learning one's lessons from them.
What person of any character would want to gain his understanding in life through someone else?"

"What if you had your heart set on learning to pilot
a plane?" Paramhansa Yogananda inquired. "Would you
object to having someone show you how?"

"Well, obviously not," replied the lady. "But I'm talking
about life situations, not artificial ones. What I mean is the
sort of circumstance in which any grown-up ought to be able
to make an adult decision."

"Such as how to dress for an outing without first checking
the weather forecast?" teased Yogananda.

"Well, . . ." hesitated the lady.

"Surely it would be foolish to go through life without
accepting advice from anyone."

"Of course," the lady agreed. "In the case of a guru, however, the disciple is forced to obey him without question, like
a robot."

"By no means!" replied Yogananda emphatically. "Any
guru who demanded mindless obedience of his disciples
would attract only mindless disciples. He would be given
a wide berth by strong-willed devotees, who alone are fit for
the path to God-realization.

"It takes great vigor, and great strength of character, to find
God. Could the shock of omnipresence be sustained by spiritual weaklings?

"No disciple is forced to obey his guru. Freedom to accept or reject is one of the first laws of the spiritual life. It is a right given to us since the time of our creation by the Lord Himself."

The Master smiled. "Just see how many people exercise their right to reject Him for incarnations! Yet the Lord is so humble, He never forces Himself on anyone. We may reject Him for eons, and the Lord, while loving us through eternity, says, 'I will wait.'

"Do you realize what you're saying when you say you are attracted to the concept, Self-realization, but reject the need for a guru? People commonly misunderstand Self-realization to mean the development of their human personality to its highest potential. But Self-realization is a soul-potential, not a human one.

"The personality is like a dense forest, beyond which lies the beautiful, expansive land that God has promised you. To reach Him, you must somehow get out of the forest, and not waste time exploring its countless lanes.

"People have no idea how to get out of their mental forest. Every path they attempt ends in a confusion of dense under-growth, or leads them back to where they first started out. In time, the realization dawns on them that they are lost.

"Then, if someone comes and says, 'I know this forest well; let me show you the way through it,' will they consider his offer a menace to their free will? Won't they view it, rather, as an opportunity to accomplish successfully what their own will has been trying for so long, but always in vain, to accomplish?

"You speak of adult decisions. In that forest, age has nothing to do with a person's ability to make decisions. Experience is what counts. Even a little child, if he knows the way, will lead you better than you can lead yourself, if you are lost. In that context, it might even be truer to say that that child is more adult than you are. At any rate, he is better able to assume responsibility for taking you where you want to go.

"All of us, before God, are but children. Life itself is a great school, and our lessons in it won't end until we've realized who we *really* are, as children of the Infinite.

"The purpose of the guru is not to weaken your will. It is to teach you secrets of developing your inner power, until you can stand unshaken amidst the crash of breaking worlds.

"To develop such divine self-reliance is a much greater accomplishment, surely, than standing 'on your own two feet' in life's everyday situations.

"People who reject the need for a guru," Paramhansa Yogananda concluded, "don't realize what a steep mountain stands before them on the path to God. To climb this mountain without a guide would be worse than foolish: Spiritually, it could prove disastrous."

2

"A gemologist can distinguish between a genuine stone and an imitation one. If you go to buy an expensive gemstone, but scorn expert advice, you may find that you've spent a great deal of money for nothing.

"A guru is like the gemologist. He can help you to avoid costly mistakes, which might otherwise set you back in your spiritual efforts for many incarnations."

3

"The labyrinth in Greek mythology was so intricate that no one, once inside it, had ever been able to find his way out again. Theseus, however, succeeded. What he did was carry a spool of twine with him and unwind it as he entered the maze. By following the string back, he found his way once more into the open.

"The guru is like that length of twine. He doesn't have to be there at every turn to tell you what to do. Even mental attunement with him will suffice. You will know, through your attunement, whether the choices you contemplate are right for you, or wrong."

⊷4⊶

"People who are still locked up in the cage of ego often view the prospect of having a guru as a threat to their personal freedom. They don't realize that freedom is exactly what they don't have at present!

"The guru's role is to open the door of the cage. If a disciple, finding himself still attached to limitation, cries, 'Leave me alone; I like my nice little nest of pleasures and desires!' the guru won't insist. He will say, simply, 'I came because you called me; otherwise I would not have troubled. It wasn't my need that brought me; it was yours. So, until you call me again, I will wait.'

"Accepting a guru isn't the assumption of a burden! It isn't a menace to a person's free will and happiness! It is the greatest blessing that you, or anyone, can possibly have in this world. Incarnations of good karma are required to attract the help of a true guru.

"God sends the seeker indirect guidance at first, through books and lesser teachers. Only when the desire for Him is very strong does He send help in the form of a Self-realized guru. It is no favor to the guru if the student accepts him. Rather, the student must have prayed very hard, in this lifetime and in former lives, to have earned so great a blessing.

"It isn't that you need to go out looking for the guru. The Lord will send him to you, or else draw you to him, when you are spiritually ready."

-»≡ 5 ≡«-

"The bond with the guru, once established, is not for one lifetime only. It is forever. Even after the disciple has attained spiritual freedom, he acknowledges the guru as the channel through which his liberation came.

"For the guru is simply a channel for God's power and wisdom. God is the true Guru.

"The guru is like a transformer, which makes a higher voltage of electricity available to ordinary households.

"Sometimes, indeed, the disciple becomes greater than the guru. Such was the case with Jesus, who was more spiritually developed than John the Baptist, although John the Baptist— as I explain in my autobiography[1]—was his guru from former incarnations. This was why John said, in humility, that Jesus ought to be baptizing him. And it was why Jesus replied, 'Suffer it to be so now: for thus it becometh us to fulfill all righteousness.'[2] It was also why Jesus said, 'Among those that are born of women there is not a greater prophet than John the Baptist.'[3] Wasn't Jesus himself born of woman? He was giving recognition, simply, to the fact that his debt as a disciple was eternal.

"Thus, you see, the bond of guru and disciple is not that of master and slave. It is an eternal bond of divine love and friendship.

"If, in the beginning, the guru disciplines his disciple, it is as that disciple's best and truest friend; as one who would help him to achieve what he most wants in his soul. Only a false guru would pamper his disciples' egos with flattery.

"A true guru never disciplines with selfish motivation. Whatever teaching or discipline he gives to the disciple comes not from himself, but from God."

❧ 6 ❧

To a certain disciple, Paramhansa Yogananda once said, "I lost touch with you for a few incarnations. But I will never lose touch with you again."

❧ 7 ❧

Of another disciple, who had rejected Yogananda as his guru: "He will never attain freedom except through this channel, sent to him by God."

❧ 8 ❧

"Master," said a disciple, "I find great joy in serving God, but it is so difficult for me to sit still in meditation!"

"Very well," the Master replied, "for now, serve Him faithfully, with devotion. I will meditate for you."

‑‑9‑‑

"All the guidance we need is contained in the Bible," argued the minister of another church. "What purpose can be served by following a guru?"

"What the Bible says," replied Paramhansa Yogananda, "and what people *understand* of what it says are often poles apart! You can misunderstand the scriptures, and they won't correct you. But the guru can point out your misunderstanding.

"The guru is a living scripture. He speaks from the same perception of Truth as that which any master attained who ever lived before him. The source of his wisdom, and theirs, is the same.

"The Bible, moreover, is not to the same degree throughout inspired by the highest wisdom. Some of those who wrote it were more enlightened than others. Some were not particularly enlightened at all. Translators, moreover, with merely human understanding, altered the meaning of certain passages—especially of those which had been written from profound, but therefore uncommon, insight.

"Even the disciples of Jesus Christ reported his words according to their own sometimes limited ability to comprehend them. We read passages in which Jesus upbraided them for the superficiality of their understanding.

"So you see, the truth in the Bible comes to us filtered, even through so great a scripture.

"The teaching in the scriptures, moreover, is for everybody. It is not particularized to the needs of the individual seeker.

"For all of these reasons, a guru is necessary.

"The most important reason for having a guru, however, is stated in the Bible itself. It says there, 'But as many as received him, to them *gave he power* to become the sons of God.'[4]

"The guru gives his disciple not only teaching and guidance: He also transmits to him spiritual power.

"As Jesus raised Lazarus from the dead, so the guru raises the disciple inwardly to the life of the Spirit. The Lord Himself, through the guru, awakens the devotee from his age-old sleep of delusion."

⇥ 10 ⇤

"Those who join us on this path of Self-realization are not connected to some printing press, but to a line of God-realized masters. God Himself, through them, overshadows this work. All who follow it sincerely, with devotion, will be brought to Him."

1 *Autobiography of a Yogi*, Chapter 35, "The Christlike Life of Lahiri Mahasaya."
2 Matthew 3:14,15.
3 Luke 7:28.
4 John 1:12.

Chapter 15

THE DISCIPLE'S PART

-⊷ 1 ⊷-

Paramhansa Yogananda said, "When I met my guru, Swami Sri Yukteswar, he said to me, 'Allow me to discipline you.'

"'Why, Sir?' I inquired.

"'When I encountered my guru, Lahiri Mahasaya,' he replied, 'my will was guided by whims. But when I attuned my will to Lahiri Mahasaya's wisdom-guided will, my own will became free, because guided by wisdom.'

"In the same way," Yogananda continued, "I discovered that by attuning my will to Sri Yukteswar's wisdom-guided will, my will, too, became free.

"This is the purpose of discipleship, and of the obedience that it entails. The aim of obedience to the guru is not to enslave the disciple, but to liberate his will from that which enslaves it truly: whims, and much more—bondage to likes and dislikes, and to desires and attachments.

"Most people consider it an affirmation of freedom to indulge their desires 'freely.' They don't see that desire itself is compulsive. It blinds their discrimination. Where is the freedom in any act that leads one more deeply into bondage?

"Spiritual healing requires willing cooperation on the disciple's part. It cannot be achieved by passivity. Surrender to the divine will, as expressed through the guru, must be offered freely, willingly, and intelligently.

"Unenlightened teachers often try to impose their will on the disciples. Freedom can never be achieved in this way, even if the advice given is essentially valid. To impose one's will on another is wrong, spiritually, like the practice of hypnosis, which weakens the will of the person hypnotized.

"Obedience must be to the highest that is in your own self. Spiritual instruction, too, must proceed from that high level of consciousness. It must be attuned to the guidance for which your own soul is longing.

"The difference between such wisdom-inspired guidance and human discrimination, based on introspection, is that the unenlightened mind is clouded by likes and dislikes, and conditioned by past habits and old ways of looking at things. The guru's consciousness, on the other hand, is like a flawless mirror. It reflects the disciple's spiritual state back to him. It gives him what he needs, to escape the bondage of delusion.

"Cooperation with the guru strengthens the will power immeasurably, for it attunes the disciple's will to the infinite will of God."

-⇒ 2 ⇐-

"Why is the new Kriya initiate required to say, 'I do,' when he comes forward to receive the blessing during the ceremony? It isn't only a promise to practice the techniques, and, in keeping with ancient tradition, to guard their secrecy. It is the 'I *will*' of discipleship. It expresses the devotee's firm resolve thenceforth to set aside ego-motivated desires, and to dedicate himself to doing God's will alone, as expressed through the line of gurus.

"If you take initiation in this spirit, you will quickly reach God."

-⇒ 3 ⇐-

"When purchasing a car, it is sensible, at first, to compare models. 'This one has such-and-such advantages,' you'll say. 'That one has such-and-such others.' Once you've reached a decision, however, your common sense ought to tell you to back it wholeheartedly. What use would be served, at that point, by further hesitation?

"Suppose you buy a Plymouth, and drive it from Los Angeles with the intention of going to Boston. On arriving in Arizona, however, you think, 'Perhaps I'd have done better to buy a Buick.' So you return, trade in your Plymouth for a Buick, and start out again. Hardly have you reached New Mexico, however, when you think, 'Maybe it should have been an Oldsmobile.' So back you go to Los Angeles to repeat the process yet a third time.

"Apart from the cost of all these changes, in both time and money, you may end up never completing your journey.

"That is how some people are: Even after accepting a guru they keep on asking themselves, 'Shall I accept what he says on this particular point? Why did he say what he did yesterday? That wasn't what *I* would have said.' And sometimes they wonder, 'Does he really know what he's doing?'

"It isn't that obedience should be stupid. It takes discrimination and deep, intuitive understanding even to know *how* to obey. Until the disciple rids himself, however, of the tendency to indulge in carping doubts, he will never establish that relationship with the guru which will take him to God."

4

"Intuition is necessary to discipleship. Otherwise, you won't understand the guru's guidance.

"Don't depend too much on your reasoning faculty. Wisdom can't be achieved by intellectualizing the truth. Nor can intuitive understanding be achieved by argument.

"Spiritual insight requires tuning in with faith to what the guru says, and to what he asks of you. Intuitive faith, not logic, is the basis of divine understanding."

⋖ 5 ⋗

"Train your mind to say instantly, 'I will!' Only then think *how* to accomplish what has been asked of you. For with too much reasoning comes hesitation, confusion, and doubt. In the end, you may find that your will power has become so paralyzed that you are incapable of acting at all."

⋖ 6 ⋗

"Some people, when sleeping, are almost impossible to wake up. You call them, and they don't answer. You shake them, and they cry, 'Leave me alone!' You shake them a little more, and they may open their eyes a little bit; they may even sit up. But the moment you leave them, they collapse back onto the bed and fall asleep again.

"There are some people, on the other hand, who respond with alert attention the moment you call them. That is the way of the true devotee. The moment God summons him, he responds eagerly and willingly. Thereafter, he never thinks back nostalgically to his former sleep of delusion, but seeks ever greater wakefulness in God.

"Be like that true devotee."

⋖ 7 ⋗

"If a doctor gives you a prescription, but you tear it up and toss it away, how can you expect to be cured?

"The guru is your spiritual 'doctor.' Do as he advises you. If you follow his 'prescription' even a little bit, your life will be transformed."

―☙ 8 ❧―

"We had a young boy here, who had come with his mother. Every time I tried to offer him a suggestion for his welfare, he would pout and cry, 'Mama, he's scolding me!' At last I simply left him alone. Why try to help a person if he doesn't want to be helped?

"But remember, if I say anything that you don't like, it isn't *you*, in your deeper reality, who are being hurt. It is only that part of you which you have come here to change, or to get rid of."

―☙ 9 ❧―

"Remember the words of Jesus, 'The last shall be first.'[1] Go on to the end of life. Those who are still there at the finish— not for 'sticking it out,' but because they love God—will be the first in the kingdom of heaven."

―☙ 10 ❧―

"Attunement to the guru means complete, heartfelt acceptance of his guidance, and also of his activities. Your acceptance must be unqualified. You mustn't say, for instance, 'I accept what the guru tells me in this situation, but not in that one.' Nor should you say, 'I accept what he tells me, but not what those say whom he has appointed to represent him.'

"Attunement means also listening for the guru's *inner* guidance, in your heart. In everything, ask him mentally what you should do; how you should behave; how you can love God more deeply. More than guidance, ask him to give you the *power* to develop spiritually.

"Be guided by common sense also. Never, in the name of attunement, behave in such a way as to offend against reason or against the rules of proper conduct. 'Learn to behave,' Sri Yukteswar used to say. Don't let attunement with the guru, in other words, be your excuse for an undisciplined imagination!"

11

"Words are incapable of conveying the fullness of an idea or a perception. Listen to my words, but try also to tune in to the deeper meaning behind them. I prefer magnetizing you with my thoughts to teaching you outwardly, through words. For only when I can touch you from within, in your consciousness, do I know that you have grasped my true meaning."

12

"To tune in to the guru's consciousness, visualize him in the spiritual eye. Mentally call to him there. Imagine his eyes, especially, gazing at you. Invite his consciousness to inspire your own.

"Then, after calling to him for some time, try to feel his response in your heart. The heart is the center of intuition in the body. It is your 'radio-receiver.'

"Your 'broadcasting station' is situated in the Christ center between the eyebrows. It is from this center that your will broadcasts into the universe your thoughts and ideas.

"Once you feel an answer in the heart, call to the guru deeply, 'Introduce me to God.'"

⇀⊶ 13 ⊶⇀

"There is a saying in the Indian scriptures, 'All of Krishna's soldiers were like Krishna.' You can tell to which ray of the divine light a person is attuned by the consciousness he expresses in his life. He gives up his little ego and assumes a new radiance, colored by the vibration, or ray, of light that he has accepted as his particular path to God.

"It isn't that he loses touch with who he is, in himself. That, one never loses. But he assumes responsibility for manifesting God in his life, instead of living in bondage to the ego with its limitations of likes and dislikes.

"Since your path is the one to which God has drawn you, you naturally express Him in that way. By attracting to yourself the guru's realization of God, you attain his state of Self-realization.

"Does it make you a carbon copy of the guru? Just see the difference, on a human level, between Sri Yukteswar and my human self. Sri Yukteswarji was a *gyani*.[2] My human nature, by contrast, inclines me rather to express divine love and joy. Yet inside, in our spirit, we are one."

⇀⊶ 14 ⊶⇀

"You must be loyal to the guru. Loyalty is the first law of God, even as treachery is the greatest sin before God. If you are loyal, moreover, show your loyalty by your words and actions.

"D— —, one of the disciples here, has always been very obliging by nature, but sometimes too much so. There was a time when she would agree with anyone on almost any subject, simply to oblige. I told her once, 'If someone were to come to you and say, "I saw Yogananda yesterday dead drunk, staggering down Main Street," you would reply, wide-eyed, "Is that so?"' I added, 'I know you wouldn't believe it, but don't you see, you must be courageous in expressing your beliefs.'

"To stand up for what you believe in is a sign of loyalty. I don't say you should be fanatical, but on the other hand don't be wishy-washy. If you would unite your soul with Him, Who is the foundation of the universe, be firm in what you stand for."

⇥15⇤

A disciple was lamenting that she didn't feel the guru's help as much as others did.

"If you shut me out," Paramhansa Yogananda replied quietly, "how can I come in?"

⇥16⇤

Yogananda taught: "The company one keeps determines to a great extent whether his energy will move inward, toward God, or outward, toward the world. Good company is essential on the spiritual path."

"Sir," asked a disciple, "what if I am alone?"

The Master gazed deeply into his eyes as he replied, "Am I not always with you?"

17

A few months before Paramhansa Yogananda left his body, this disciple asked him, "Sir, when we can no longer see you physically, will you still be as near to us as you are now?"

With deep seriousness the Master replied, "To those who *think* me near, I will be near."

1   Matthew 19:30.
2   A sage; one who manifests God in His aspect of wisdom.

Chapter 16

WAYS IN WHICH GOD CAN BE WORSHIPED

-»» 1 ««-

"I am intrigued by the concept of Self-realization," said a college student, whose major was in philosophy. "However, I don't see how you tie it in with worship. Surely it isn't your teaching that we should worship ourselves!"

"But isn't that what everyone does?" asked Paramhansa Yogananda with a humorous smile. "That is the very essence of delusion: to idolize the ego; to pour out libations to it, pamper it, sing praises to it!

"Worship means to seek identity with the object of one's concentration. On the path of Self-realization, the devotee seeks to transfer his identity from the little ego to the infinite Self. Philosophically, then, it is valid to worship that greater Self.

"This is a difficult concept, however, for the human mind to grasp. One may affirm, 'I am infinite,' but without humility and devotion one slips all too easily into the error of thinking, 'I, in my exceptional greatness, am one with Infinity!'

"For this reason it is better, until one is highly advanced spiritually, not to think of God as, 'I,' but to address Him as, 'Thou.' It is also more natural to think in this way. After all, as human beings we see others as separate from ourselves, even though, spiritually speaking, all are manifestations of the one divine Self. We don't ask a friend how he is by saying, 'How am I today?' To do so would be confusing even for a philosopher! Instead, we say, 'How are *you*?'

"An 'I-and-Thou' relationship with God is simpler, and less confusing. It is also much more satisfying to the human mind. And it is a relationship that God recognizes.

"The Lord responds to sincere devotion from His human children, never to proud self-affirmation."

-->~2~<--

"Steam is invisible," Yogananda said, "but when cooled it becomes visible as water. Water, when cooled further still, becomes ice. Steam and water are without form, but ice can be formed into countless different shapes.

"The Infinite Lord, similarly, is invisible behind His creation, even though, like the steam in a steam engine, it is His power that makes everything function. By our devotion, however, we may 'condense' Him into visibility as the inner light, beheld in meditation. By still deeper meditation, our devotion's 'frost' may 'freeze' Him and cause Him to appear to us in actual form.

"Thus, the Infinite Lord has appeared to many devotees as their Heavenly Father, or their Divine Mother, or in countless other aspects that their hearts held dear."

-->~3~<--

A scientist once challenged Paramhansa Yogananda: "Considering the vastness of the universe, with its countless billions of galaxies, surely it is superstitious to believe that the Creator of this immensity listens to our prayers."

"Your conception of Infinity is too finite!" rejoined the Master with ready wit. "Although the Lord is infinitely vast, He is also, in His infinity, infinitesimal.

"Infinity means, 'without end.' The infinity of God's consciousness goes not only outward, but inward—to the very heart of the atom. He is as conscious of every human thought, of every feeling, as He is of the movements of vast galaxies in space."

~➣⊙ 4 ⊙⊱~

A student of comparative religion posed the Master a dilemma he'd encountered in his studies. "I find," he said, "that every religion defines God differently. It makes me wonder if the founders of the world's great religions really knew what they were talking about!"

Paramhansa Yogananda replied with a smile, "Your mind has been conditioned to think that defining a thing is the same thing as understanding it. No definition could ever encompass God.

"An architect, upon returning from a visit to London, might describe the city in terms of the buildings he'd seen. A gardener, having viewed all the same sights, might describe the city's parks. A politician might speak of the needs of the people of London. None would be able to convey the actual experience of visiting that city.

"Take another example: How would you explain the taste of an orange to someone who had never tasted one? You could never do so adequately.

"The goal of religion is not to define God accurately. It is to inspire in people the desire to commune with Him—to experience Him in inner silence, in their souls.

"The founders of the great religions spoke from that inner experience. When they sought to explain God, they did so in terms that they hoped would touch their listeners.

"Thus, sometimes they described Him as their Beloved; again, as a mighty King; and again, as a great Light. Jesus spoke of Him as his Heavenly Father. Buddha didn't speak of Him at all, lest the people of his time continue their passive dependence on God's help.

"No master is concerned with formulating absolute definitions. What he hopes, simply, is to convey a suggestion of the divine experience.

"Thus, if sometimes he compares it to the drinking of wine, or to the pleasures of human love, it is only because he wants to inspire people to seek perfection beyond the things of earth. Since at present they feel attracted to these things, he says to them, 'In ecstasy you will find a joy that is infinitely superior to everything you now enjoy.'"

⟶ 5 ⟵

A Hindu student in America once laughingly told Paramhansa Yogananda, "My grandmother in India listens to *bhajans* [devotional songs] on the radio. At the end of the singing, she places a flower on it as a devotional offering—as if the radio were a holy image!"

The Master smiled at this encounter between scientific materialism and traditional piety. "And yet," he commented, "your grandmother is not so superstitious as she seems. For with the flower she is expressing her gratitude to God. It isn't that she views the radio as a deity. She is simply seeking an external focus for her devotion.

"And isn't it good to see God enshrined everywhere? We think of the radio as man-made, but from Whom came the intelligence that made the radio? From Whom came even the materials from which it was created?

"When we seek to remove God from our environment, it becomes all too easy for us to remove Him from our lives altogether."

·➺·6·➻·

"One thing I cannot appreciate in the Hindu religion," said a Christian severely, "is its plethora of gods."

"There are many," agreed the Master. "Each, however, represents an attempt to remind us of God in one of His innumerable aspects. They are abstractions—a way of saying, 'No human being can really understand what God *is*, but here, at least, is something that He *does*.'

"Take, for example, the image of the goddess Kali. This is a good case in point, because, out of all Hindu images, Kali has been the one most misunderstood by Western minds.

"Kali stands naked. Her right foot is placed on the chest of Her prostrate husband. Her hair streams out, disheveled, behind Her. A garland of human heads adorns Her neck. In one of four hands She brandishes a sword; in another, a severed head. Her tongue, usually painted a bright red, lolls out as though in blood-lust."

At this point the Christian shuddered. Yogananda grinned roguishly.

"If we thought that this image depicted Kali as She is," he continued, "I grant you, it might awaken devotion in very few devotees! However, the purpose of that image is to describe certain universal functions of the Divine in Nature.

"Kali represents Mother Nature. She is *Aum*, the cosmic vibration. In *Aum* everything exists—all matter, all energy, and the thoughts of all conscious beings. Hence, Her garland of heads, to show that She is invisibly present in all minds.

"The play of life and death expresses Her activity in Nature: creation, preservation, and destruction. Hence the sword, the head, and a third hand extended, bestowing life.

"Her energy is omnipresent; hence Her streaming hair, representing energy.

"Shiva, Her husband, represents God in His vibrationless state, beyond creation. Thus, He is depicted as supine.

"Kali's tongue is protruding not in blood-lust as most people believe, but because in India, when a person makes a mistake, he sticks out his tongue. In the West, don't you express embarrassment somewhat similarly? You put your hands to your mouth.

"Kali is depicted as dancing all over creation. This dance represents the movement of cosmic vibration, in which all things exist. When Kali's foot touches the breast of the Infinite, however, She puts her tongue out as if to say, 'Oh, oh, I've gone too far!' For at the touch of the Infinite Spirit, all vibration ceases.

"Kali's fourth hand is raised in blessing on those who seek, not Her gifts, but liberation from the endless play of *maya*, or delusion.

"Those who feel themselves attracted to Nature's outward manifestations must continue the endless round of life and death, through incarnation after incarnation. Those devotees, however, who deeply long for freedom from the cosmic play worship God in the indwelling Self. Through meditation, they merge in the infinite *Aum*. And from oneness with *Aum* they pass beyond creation, to unite their consciousness with God—timeless, eternal Bliss.

"The statues of Kali are not intended to depict the Divine Mother as She looks, but simply to display Her functions in the aspect of Mother Nature.

"The Divine Mother is, of course, without form, though we may say also that Her body is the entire universe, with its infinity of suns and moons. She can also appear to the devotee in human form, however. When She does so, She is enshrined in supernal beauty.

"All the images of gods in India are symbolic. We must look beyond their shapes to the hidden meanings they represent."

-»●● 7 ●●«-

"I have trouble visualizing God," complained a student of religious New Thought. "I've imagined Him as Infinite Intelligence, as the I AM principle, as my God-Self within, as the Cosmic Ground of Being. It all seems so abstract! But your relationship with the Lord is so loving. How can I achieve such a relationship?"

"The first step," replied the Master, "is not to imagine that He wants your definitions. He wants only your love.

"Why not," Yogananda then suggested, "worship the Infinite as your Divine Mother?"

"What a lovely idea!" exclaimed the visitor. "But is it valid? Is it true?"

"Indeed, yes!" replied Sri Yogananda emphatically. "God's love is already reflected in human relationships. His love, like the sunlight shining on countless pieces of glass, is reflected everywhere.

"The Infinite is the Mother behind all human mothers, the true Father behind all human fathers. He is the ever-loyal Friend behind all earthly friends. He is the eternal Beloved behind all human loves. He is all things to all men, because, you see, the Lord is everything.

"Through your parents He cares for you, supports you, and protects you. Through your friends He shows you that love is a free sharing, without any hint of compulsion. Through the beloved He helps one to find the selfless intensity of divine love. Through people's children He helps them to understand love as something precious, as a thing to be protected from harmful influences and nourished with devotion.

"Countless are the forms in which God comes to man. In each, He seeks to teach man something of His infinite nature. The lessons are there, for anyone whose heart is open to receive them.

"Thus, it isn't that the Lord wants you to deny your human nature. What He wants, rather, is for you to purify it: to expand whatever love you feel in your heart, and not to keep it locked up in ego-attachments.

"For the devotee, it is natural therefore to worship God in some human aspect: as his Divine Mother, for example, or as his Heavenly Father.

"I myself worship the Mother aspect, especially. For the Mother is closer than the Father. The Father aspect of God represents that part which is aloof from His creation. The Mother is creation itself. Even among mankind, the human father is more disposed than the mother to judge their erring children. The mother always forgives.

"Pray, then, to the Divine Mother. Talk to Her like a child: 'Divine Mother, naughty or good, I am Your own. You *must* release me from this delusion.' The Mother ever responds with compassion when the devotee prays to Her sincerely in this way.

"Of course, in the highest sense God is none of the forms in which people worship Him. But it is helpful to use human concepts as a means of deepening our devotion to Him.

"Beyond devotion comes divine love. In that perfection of love there is complete union. In that state the yogi realizes the supreme truth: 'I am That.'"

8

"You should not be too personal in your love for God. To be personal is to remain limited by ego-consciousness. But love for Him must take one beyond the ego. If you visualize God with form, and even if you behold Him ecstatically in visions, try to see expressed in those eyes the consciousness of infinity.

"The Divine Mother is so beautiful! But remember, in Her higher manifestation even that beauty is formless. She is in everything. Her divine, compassionate love is expressed in the raindrops. Her beauty is reflected in the colors of the rainbow. She offers fresh hope to mankind with the rose-tinted clouds at dawn.

"Above all, be ever conscious of Her presence in your heart."

⟿9⟾

"There are two ways of approaching God in Nature. One is to separate the Lord from all His manifestations. '*Neti, neti,*' is the saying in India: 'Not this, not that.' Something of that consciousness there must always be, lest one become trapped in attachment to form.

"The other way is to behold the Lord manifested everywhere.

"The first way, by itself, may be too austere for most devotees. The second way is much sweeter. Best of all is a combination of both.

"The Divine Mother is busy with Her housework of creation. The baby devotee cries, and She gives him a toy to play with—riches, perhaps, or name, or fame. If he cries again, She gives him another toy. But if the baby throws everything away and cries for Her love alone, She picks him up at last and whispers to him lovingly, 'If you really want only Me, and not My gifts, then come. Be with Me forever on My lap of infinity.'"

⸻10⸻

"I find it difficult to pray to God with form," said a visiting professor. "What inspires me, rather, is the thought of vastness—infinity! When I go out under the stars at night, I think, 'How wonderful!' Truth is so grand. How unimportant, at such times, seems my little life with its petty worries and afflictions. My spirit soars in the thought of infinite space, eternity!"

"Such thoughts should be held by everyone seeking God," replied Sri Yogananda. "Always, in whatever aspect you worship Him, your sight should be focused on infinity.

"It isn't necessary to think of God with form. It depends on a person's nature. Some people find more devotional inspiration, just as you do, in a formless reality. Devotion must not be confused with sentiment. Rather, devotion is the sincere aspiration of the human heart toward the center of infinite truth."

⸻11⸻

A visitor asked the Master, "Why, when referring to God, do you use the pronoun, 'He'? Is God really masculine?"

"God is both masculine and feminine," Yogananda replied. "He also is neither masculine nor feminine. When I use the pronoun, 'He,' it isn't to limit God.

"But would people be inspired to love God if they thought of Him as 'It'? The personal pronoun suggests a conscious Being, to whom they can relate individually. The masculine pronoun, moreover, is also impersonal.

"Westerners, besides, are accustomed to thinking of God as the Father, for that is how Jesus spoke of Him."

─→ 12 ←─

"There are eight aspects in which God can be experienced: as Light, Sound, Peace, Calmness, Love, Joy, Wisdom, and Power.

"To experience Him as Light during meditation brings calmness to the mind, purifying it and giving it clarity. The more deeply one contemplates the inner light, the more one perceives all things as made of that light.

"To experience God as Sound is to commune with the Holy Ghost, or *Aum*, the Cosmic Vibration. When you are immersed in *Aum*, nothing can touch you. *Aum* raises the mind above the delusions of human existence, into the pure skies of divine consciousness.

"Peace is an early meditative experience. Peace, like a weightless waterfall, cleanses the mind of all anxiety and care, bestowing heavenly relief.

"Calmness is another divine experience. This aspect of God is more dynamic and more powerful than that of Peace. Calmness gives the devotee power to overcome all the obstacles in his life. Even in human affairs, the person who can remain calm under all circumstances is invincible.

"Love is another aspect of God—not personal love, but Love infinite. Those who live in ego-consciousness think of impersonal love as cold and abstract. But divine love is all-absorbing, and infinitely comforting. It is impersonal only in the sense that it is utterly untainted by selfish desire. The unity one finds in divine love is possible only to the soul. It cannot be experienced by the ego.

"Joy is another aspect of God. Divine joy is like millions of earthly joys crushed into one. The quest for human happiness is like looking around for a candle while sitting out of doors in the sun. Divine joy surrounds us eternally, yet people look to mere things for their happiness. Mostly, all they find is relief from emotional or physical pain. But divine joy is the blazing Reality. Before it, earthly joys are but shadows.

"Wisdom is intuitive insight, not intellectual understanding. The difference between human and divine wisdom is that the human mind comes at things indirectly, from without. The scientist, for example, investigates the atom objectively. But the yogi *becomes* the atom. Divine perception is always from within. From within alone can a thing be understood in its true essence.

"Power, finally, is that aspect of God which creates and runs the universe. Imagine what power it took to bring the galaxies into existence! Masters manifest some of that power in their lives. The expression, 'Gentle Jesus, meek and mild,' describes only one side of Jesus' nature. The other side was revealed in the power with which he drove the money-changers from the temple. Just think what magnetism it took to combat single-handedly all those men, entrenched as they were in habits and desires that had been sanctioned by ancient custom!

"People are often appalled by the power they see expressed in the lives of saints. But remember, you will never find God until you are very strong in yourself. Power may exercise less appeal on your mind than other aspects of God, but it is important to realize that divine power, too, is a part of your divine nature.

"Whatever aspect of God you experience in meditation, never keep it contained in the little chalice of your consciousness, but try always to expand that experience to infinity."

⊷13⊶

"Don't be formal with God. Play with Him. Tease Him if you like. Scold Him if you feel to—though always with love. Remember, He is your very own. He is the Nearest of the near, the Dearest of the dear. He is closer to you than the very thoughts with which you pray to Him."

Chapter 17

HOW TO PRAY EFFECTIVELY

— 1 —

"When you pray to God, pray from your heart. Say what you really feel, not what you think He wants you to say or feel. Be completely sincere with Him. He knows anyway what you are thinking! But heartfelt prayer lends power to your thoughts. It focuses them, and centers them in Him. Without sincerity, that focus will be lacking.

"If you feel no devotion, then pray to Him, 'Lord, help me to love You.'

"If your heart is restless with desires, pray to Him, 'Lord, I have these desires, but I want You more than anything else. Help me to dissolve every limitation in Your great ocean of peace.'

"It is all right to pray to God for things. It is better still, however, to ask that His will be done in your life. He knows what you need, and will do much more for you than the best that you can imagine for yourself.

"Above all, seek Him for Himself, for His love. Pray to Him, 'Father, reveal Thyself!' If you call to Him in that way, sincerely, He will be with you always."

— 2 —

"Never pray with the attitude of a beggar. You are God's child. As His child, you have a right to the treasure from His storehouse of infinity.

"Pray with utter confidence that He is listening. For indeed, so He will, if you pray to Him with love. Pray from your heart, with deep intensity.

"Demand of Him lovingly; never beg. By *demand* I don't mean you should try to force your will on Him, as though anticipating His reluctance to accede to your wishes.

I mean, pray with the firm conviction that He *wants* to give you everything you need, and that He *will* give it.

"Jesus put it this way: 'Pray believing.'[1]

"Utter faith, and love: these are the most important elements in prayer."

→⇒ 3 ⇐←

"Pray thus to God:

"'My Infinite Beloved, I know that Thou art nearer than these words with which I pray; nearer even than my nearest thoughts.

"'Behind my every restless feeling, may I feel Thy concern for me, and Thy love.

"'Behind my awareness, may I feel sustained and guided by Thy consciousness.

"'Behind my love for Thee, may I become ever more deeply conscious of Thy love.'

"If you continuously pray to Him in this way, and if you pray with all sincerity, you will feel His presence suddenly as a great joy in your heart. In that bursting joy you will know that He is with you, and that He is your very own."

⊷⊷ 4 ⊷⊷

"Pray with ecstasy. Meditate with ecstasy. And whenever you have a free moment, think of God.

"Be like the needle of a compass which, no matter which way it is turned, always points back to the north. That is the way of the yogi: No matter where he goes or what he does, his mind ever points toward the polestar of God's presence within."

⊷⊷ 5 ⊷⊷

"How should you love God? Love Him as the miser loves money; as the drowning man yearns for breath; as the desert wanderer craves water. Love Him with the first love of true lovers.

"When you have learned to love Him with all your heart, you will have Him. You will then be a yogi—one who is united with God.

"Union with the Cosmic Beloved is the most enjoyable experience possible. It is dream after dream, joy after joy; a thousand million divine romances in one, ever thrilling your heart. In every point of space you behold searchlights of His love, shining like a million suns. As often as you think you have exhausted His love, again and again, like a rolling surf, it crashes anew upon the shores of your mind.

"*That* is ecstasy!"

—6—

"God answers all prayers, but restless prayers He answers only a little bit.

"If you try to give someone something that doesn't belong to you, your gift won't mean much to him, will it? However touching the gesture, it will be lacking in substance!

"So is it when your mind is not your own. You may want to give it to God, but you can't. Your prayers, then, are hardly more than a gesture.

"Get control over your mind. When you can pray with concentration, the Lord will know that you mean what you are saying. He will answer you, then, in wonderful ways."

—7—

One of the new monks permitted his spiritual fervor to carry him into emotional outbursts in meditation. Some of the other disciples cautioned him against excessiveness in his devotion. In front of the others one day this monk handed the Master a note asking whether it was all right to pray so fervently.

"By all means it is all right!" Yogananda replied. "Roll on the floor at night and cry for God to come. One must yearn for Him, or He will never manifest Himself."

—8—

At the same time the Master cautioned, "Never pray for outward effect. If you do so, the true purpose of prayer will be lost.

"It is a common failing among devotees to seek to impress others by showing off their devotion to God. They should strive, rather, to impress the Lord!

"That is the danger of loud prayer, unless it is practiced to increase the fervor of one's devotion. Spiritual realization, no matter how wonderful, loses intensity when it is manifested outwardly. Your hunger for God should be expressed above all in inner silence."

9

"'Praise the Lord!' Whenever I hear that expression, I think of God as a rich, pampered lady!

"He doesn't want our praise. He wants our love."

10

"Should one thank God for His gifts?" a student asked.

"Thank Him, rather, for His love," replied the Master.

---

1   "And all things, whatsoever ye shall ask in prayer, believing, ye shall receive." (Matthew 21:22)

Chapter 18

ON MEDITATION

-❧ 1 ❧-

"The soul loves to meditate, for in contact with the Spirit lies its greatest joy. If, then, you experience mental resistance during meditation, remember that reluctance to meditate comes from the ego; it doesn't belong to the soul."

-❧ 2 ❧-

"The devotee who makes the supreme effort is the one who finds God. Not the one who keeps seeking excuses, saying, 'Let me find a quiet place; then I'll meditate.' Procrastinators will never reach God. But if you tell yourself, 'Right *now* I will go deep in meditation!' you can be there in an instant.

"When a person is really sleepy, can't he fall asleep anywhere? So is it with the person who loves God. He can meditate even in a train station or in the market place."

-❧ 3 ❧-

"One who wants to be a concert pianist will practice at the piano twelve hours a day. If, instead, his practice consists of pecking half-heartedly at the keys for a few minutes every day, he'll never become any good as a pianist.

"That's how it is with the search for God. How can you expect to know Him if you only half try?

"It is very difficult to reach God. If even a concert pianist must work hard to become successful in his profession, how much more earnestly must the devotee 'work' at meditation in order to realize the Infinite!

"Here, however, is an encouraging thought: Everyone who makes a sincere effort on the spiritual path will surely reach his goal. You cannot say that of worldly ambition. Not everyone can become a famous pianist, no matter how hard he tries. For in every field there is room at the top for very few. All men, however, can claim their sonship equally with the Heavenly Father."

"To meditate a short time with depth is better than to meditate for long hours with the mind running wild.

"In the beginning, therefore, don't force yourself to sit for a long time. Strive for shorter, but deeper, meditations. Then gradually, as you become accustomed to going deep, lengthen the time you sit in meditation."

5

"Don't feel badly if you find yourself too restless to meditate deeply. Calmness will come in time, if you practice regularly. Just never accept the thought that meditation is not for you. Remember, calmness is your eternal, true nature."

6

"In meditation, try to go beyond thinking. As long as thoughts enter the mind, you are functioning on the conscious level.

"When dreaming, you are in subconsciousness; then you are more aware in the astral body.

"When your consciousness withdraws still more deeply, into superconsciousness, then you are centered in bliss, in the spine. In that bliss-state you are aware in the causal body, the soul."

7

A devotee was having difficulty remaining awake during meditation. To him, Yogananda made this suggestion: "Squeeze your eyes shut several times, then open them wide and stare straight ahead. Repeat this practice once or twice more. If you do this, sleepiness will cease to bother you."

8

"While meditating, don't concentrate on the results of meditation. Meditate, rather, to please God. If you seek results, you will be disappointed if they don't come.

"In the Bhagavad Gita, Krishna counsels action without desire for the fruits of action. Meditation, too, should be approached in this spirit.

"Meditate without attachment to the fruits of meditation."

⊶9⊷

A disciple was digging a cesspool at the Master's desert retreat. He kept on digging all day long, without stopping to see how far he had come. That evening, to his amazement, he found that he had dug a deep hole.

When Paramhansa Yogananda saw what he had accomplished, he said approvingly, "That is how the devotee must seek God—continually digging, digging, without looking to see how far he has come. Then one day, suddenly, he will find himself there!

"As Lahiri Mahasaya used to tell his disciples, '*Banat, banat, ban jai!*—doing, doing, at last done!'"

⊶10⊷

"Do not expect a spiritual blossom every day in the garden of your life. Have faith that the Lord, if you surrender yourself to Him completely, will bring you divine fulfillment in His time, which is the right time.

"Having sown the seed of God-aspiration, water it daily with prayer and right action. Remove from your mind the weeds of lethargy, doubt, and indecision. When the sprouts of divine perception appear, tend them with devotional care.

"One morning you will behold, fully grown, the fairest flower of Self-realization."

→ 11 ←

"Why can't I behold the visions you do, Master?" asked a disciple, distressed with herself.

"It is the disturbance of past karma, creating hidden waves of restlessness deep in your subconsciousness. Once that karma has been worked out, your inner vision will be clear."

→ 12 ←

"Where motion ceases," the Master said, "God begins."

→ 13 ←

A disciple was having difficulty with his meditations. He asked Sri Yogananda, "Am I not trying hard enough?"

The Master answered, "You are trying too hard. You are using too much will power. It becomes nervous. Just be relaxed and natural.

"As long as you *try* to meditate, you won't be able to, just as you can't sleep so long as you *will* yourself to sleep. Will power should be used gradually. Otherwise, it may become detrimental. That's why it is better, in the beginning, to emphasize relaxation."

⟶14⟵

"Do not get excited or impatient in your efforts to find God. Be wholehearted, but not anxious about getting results. Be patient. Move toward your divine goal ever calmly, with tranquillity."

⟶15⟵

"Meditate more and more deeply, until calmness and joy become second nature to you.

"To be ecstatic is not difficult. It is *thinking* that it is difficult that holds you apart from it. Never think of divine joy as distant from you, and it will be with you always."

⟶16⟵

Paramhansa Yogananda told the monks, "Memorize my poem, *Samadhi*, and repeat it daily. It will help to awaken within you that lost memory of what you are in reality: sons of Infinity."

⟶17⟵

"Visualize your consciousness expanding like a blue light, encompassing all space. Imagine the stars and galaxies shining like the lights of a distant city within the infinitude of your being. Meditate on your vastness within.

"You will find in this visualization an important adjunct to the meditation techniques. It will help to remind you of your inner, divine nature."

⇢ 18 ⇠

"Try to feel, when walking out of doors, that everything around you is part of your own expanded awareness.

"Behold the leaves trembling on the trees, and try to feel their movement. Imagine in that movement that God is expressing His thoughts and inspirations.

"Watch the meadow grasses as they wave in the wind. Imagine the breeze as God's breath blowing over the world, inspiring all beings and giving them life.

"Listen to the birds singing. Feel that God, through their songs, is trying to reach you with feelings of divine gladness.

"Be aware of the sun's rays on your skin. Think of the heat you feel from the sun as God's energy. Let it fill your body with vitality and power. Imagine divine energy, through the sunlight, strengthening creatures everywhere on earth."

⇢ 19 ⇠

"Master," said a disciple, "I am afraid to go breathless in meditation. What can I do to overcome this limitation?"

"What you are facing is a normal obstacle on the path," replied Yogananda. "'False notion,' it is called. You are fearing something that, to the soul, is perfectly natural: deep stillness within.

"Your mind is like a bird that has been locked in a cage for many years. It fears liberty. Yet, freedom is its birthright.

"Someone opens the door to let the bird out. It may hop outside a short distance, but then suddenly it thinks, 'Oh, this vast world!' Terrified, it hops hurriedly back into its cage again.

"Gradually, then, by repeated sorties, the bird becomes accustomed to being outside its cage. Then at last, one day, it spreads its wings and soars up into the sky, free at last! And why is it free? Quite simply, because it has finally accepted freedom as its natural state.

"So it is with the devotee when he first experiences soul-freedom. But remember, as it is natural for the bird to fly up into the sky, so is it natural for the soul to soar in omnipresence."

–┉❂ 20 ❂┉–

"Just behind the darkness of closed eyes shines the light of God. When you behold that light in meditation, hold onto it with devotional zeal. Feel yourself inside it: That is where God dwells.

"If, on the other hand, you behold no light in meditation, then concentrate at the point between the eyebrows, and gaze deeply into the darkness that you see with closed eyes. Try, by your devotion, to penetrate that thick veil.

"In time you will surely behold the inner light, for it is ever there, shining in your forehead. Just as all human beings have eyes, so does everyone have this spiritual eye within his forehead. It awaits only his discovery in deep concentration within."

⊸ 21 ⊸

"A bent spine is the enemy of realization. In meditation, always hold your spine straight, that the life-force may flow through it unobstructed.

"Next, hold your attention fixed at the Christ center between the eyebrows. The more deeply you concentrate at that point, the more you will find your ego dissolving in superconsciousness."

⊸ 22 ⊸

"If you want to be a Master in this lifetime," Yogananda told a disciple, "then, along with your other meditation practices, practice *Hong-Sau*[1] at least two hours a day.

"As a boy, I used to practice *Hong-Sau* sometimes for seven hours at a time, until I entered the breathless state of ecstasy."

⊸ 23 ⊸

"Practice Kriya Yoga[2] so deeply that breath becomes mind. For the breath is only a gross dream, from which you will awake someday in superconsciousness."

-•=24=•-

"If you eat your dinner and then run, you won't be able to enjoy what you've eaten; you may only get indigestion. But if you rest afterwards, you will find that this is the best time to enjoy the effects of your meal.

"Follow the same practice after finishing Kriya Yoga. Don't jump up immediately, but sit still for a long time—as long as you can do so comfortably. Pray to God deeply. Practice *Bhakti* Yoga, or devotion. Or watch the flow of breath in the spine while practicing *Hong-Sau*. Or listen to the inner sounds with open ears."

-•=25=•-

A disciple asked, "How can intuition be developed?"

Yogananda: "The best way is, every time you meditate, to sit calmly for a long time after doing the techniques. It is during this period that you will be able to deepen your awareness of God's presence within you. Go ever deeper in your enjoyment of that presence.

"The longer and more deeply you enjoy the peace within, the more quickly will your intuition develop."

❧ 26 ❧

Once, after a meditation at his desert retreat, Yogananda said to the disciples who were present, "This is the kingdom of OM.[3] Listen! It is not enough merely to hear OM. You must merge yourself in that inner sound.

"OM is Divine Mother. OM Kali! OM Kali! OM Kali! Listen: Oh, how beautiful it is! OM Kali! OM Kali! OM Kali!"

---

1   A yoga technique taught by the Master.
2   See Chapter 13, "The Highway to the Infintie."
3   AUM, the Cosmic Vibration. OM is an alternative spelling. In this volume I have generally adhered to the former spelling, as it is more correct. In the above saying, however, the Master was uttering this sound as a chant. I have spelled it OM, therefore, to give the reader a clearer sense of how the word should be pronounced. —*ed*

Chapter 19

GENERAL COUNSEL

—∎ 1 ∎—

"Live in this world as a guest. Your true home is not here. The deed to the house you live in may be written in your name, but whose was it before you acquired it? And whose will it be after you die? It is only a wayside inn, a brief halting place on the long journey to your home in God.

"Think of yourself, then, as a guest on earth. Of course, as long as you are here, try to be a good guest. Be on your best behavior. Act responsibly. Take care of the things God has given you to use. Never forget for a moment, however, that they are His, not your own.

"How foolish people are to devote all their time to pampering their bodies, to accumulating wealth, to amassing more possessions! When death slaps them, they will have to leave everything behind.

"People make endless excuses. 'I have no time for meditation,' they cry. 'I have all these appointments to keep.' Well, when God calls them they'll have to break every other engagement! Death is the one 'appointment' they can't cancel.

"Why waste so much time on things that are not lasting? O blind ones: Wake up!

"God calls to you from beyond life's little pleasures. He calls to you from beyond pain, pleasure's twin. 'Seek Me,' He calls. 'Find in Me the changeless joy that you've sought so long on the waves of change. All that you've wanted for incarnations you shall find forever in Me alone.'"

―⊷ 2 ⊶―

"Reflect always that you belong to no one, and no one belongs to you. You are on this earth for but a little while, and your real reason for being here is very different from what you've imagined.

"Your family claims you as its own, but if you die and are reborn next door, will they recognize you?

"Your friends claim you as theirs, but if you cease in some way to please them, even through some trivial misunderstanding, how many of them will remain loyal to you?

"People say that they love others, but in fact they love themselves. For they love others insofar as others please *them.*

"Real love is that which finds happiness, even at the cost of great personal sacrifice, in the happiness of the one loved. How many people love in that way? So few! And of those few, how many find their love reciprocated? Fewer still!

"Only our love for God is ever fully requited—indeed, far more than requited. For God understands us when all others misunderstand. God loves us when others turn against us. God remembers us when everyone forgets us. We are God's, and God's alone, for all eternity."

―⊷ 3 ⊶―

"A good rule to follow in life is to be 'other'-minded. Here is what I mean:

"No matter what you behold, try to be conscious of that 'other,' greater reality behind what you are beholding.

"No matter with whom you are speaking, imagine that 'other' One, communicating with you through that person's words and gestures.

"Whatever work you are doing, feel that 'other' Presence nearby, watching you, guiding you, giving you strength.

"When looking into people's eyes, see God there, touching you through their consciousness.

"With every event in your life, watch it as it unfolds. Ask yourself, 'What is God trying to teach me through this experience?'"

4

"No matter what happens, look at life with non-attachment.

"Consider the example of people who go to the movies. The more suspenseful the plot, the more likely they are to come away saying, 'What a great movie!' If the plot was a tragedy, they may reflect, 'I am grateful. I learned so much from that story.' If the hero got caught in embarrassing situations, they may laugh appreciatively at his discomfiture.

"And yet, later on, when they find themselves in an embarrassing situation, are they able to laugh at the humor of it? And when tragedy strikes, are they as grateful for the lessons they learn from it? Not most of them, certainly. Their philosophy of life can be understood from the popular expression, 'Better him than me!'

"Be detached inwardly from whatever happens in your life. Thus, you will gradually free yourself from identification with this dream world, and become conscious of your oneness with the Dreamer."

-»=◉ 5 ◉=«-

"If you want to escape ego-bondage, learn to be more impersonal where your own feelings are concerned. Love for God too easily becomes personal in the human sense. When it does so, you give emphasis to the very ego you need to transcend, in order to find Him.

"Therefore it is better to seek God for bliss, primarily, and only secondarily for love, lest your love for Him fall short of that impersonal quality which is the essence of divine love.

"Radha was a great devotee of Krishna. But once she fell briefly into the delusion of personal love. The thought entered her mind that she completely owned Krishna. Soon afterward they were walking together in the forest. Radha said, 'I am very tired.'

"'Oh?' replied Krishna. 'Would you like me to carry you?' She was so pleased! Krishna lifted her onto his back. Just then, as she was thinking how pleasant it was to be carried by him, she found herself on the ground. Krishna had vanished into thin air!

"As long as she held that attitude of possessiveness, you see, he could exist no more for her.

"Immediately realizing her mistake, Radha knelt on the ground and prayed, 'Lord, I beseech your pardon.'

"Krishna reappeared as if nothing had happened. And together they continued their walk through the forest."

-»=◉ 6 ◉=«-

"Those who love others selflessly are already on the way to learning the secret of divine devotion. All they need is to direct that love upward, to God.

"Radha was the greatest of the gopis.[1] Krishna felt free, therefore, to demonstrate his selfless, divine love for her, though in reality he gave that love equally to all.

"There came a time when the other gopis grew jealous of Radha. Krishna decided to teach them a lesson.

"One day Radha happened to be absent, but the other gopis were all clustered about him. Suddenly with a groan he cried, 'Oh! Oh! I have a terrible headache! Please, won't someone do something for me?'

"'What, Lord?' they cried in desperation. 'What can we do? We'll do anything!'

"'If only one of you will press her feet on my head, my headache will go away.'

"The gopis gasped in horror. In India, to place one's feet on the head of someone senior to oneself is considered insulting. To place them on the head of the guru is sacrilegious. In deep consternation the gopis looked away. None dared to offer her services.

"And all the while, Krishna's headache kept growing worse.

"After some time had passed, Radha appeared. She learned of Krishna's distress. 'What can I do to help, Lord?' she cried anxiously, as the others had done.

"'Please, just press your feet on my head!' Krishna cried. 'Nothing else will help me.'

"'But of course, Lord. Instantly!' replied Radha.

"'No! No! You mustn't!' cried the other gopis.

"'Why on earth not?' inquired Radha.

"'If you do,' they warned her, 'you will go to hell!'

"'Is that all that's worrying you?' Radha scoffed. 'Why, if pressing my feet on our Lord's head will give him one moment of relief, I will gladly go to hell for eternity!'

"She was about to do as he had asked, when Krishna sat up smiling. His headache was gone.

"And then the other gopis understood. They had been concentrating on their own safety, not on Krishna's well-being. Now they all bowed before Radha's greater, because selfless, love."

--- 7 ---

A visitor asked Paramhansa Yogananda, "Is renunciation necessary on the spiritual path?"

"Yes!" declared the Master emphatically. "Whether married or single, one should always feel in his heart that God is his one true Beloved, Who alone resides in the temple of all human hearts.

"Renunciation means, above all, non-attachment. It is not how you live outwardly that matters, but how you live within.

"Make your heart a hermitage, I always say, and your robe your love for God."

--- 8 ---

"Never let the thought enter your mind that you own anything. Whenever I see someone who needs something of mine more than I do, I gladly give it to him."

--- 9 ---

"If you want to feel God's guidance in your life, don't waste time talking idly with others. Silence is the altar of the Spirit."

⟶10⟵

"When you are with others, be with them wholeheartedly. But when you are by yourself, be alone with God. Spend ever more time with Him."

⟶11⟵

"Seclusion is the price of greatness."

⟶12⟵

"The company you keep is important. If you leave your coat in a room where people are smoking, pretty soon it will smell of smoke. If you leave it outside in the garden, later on, when you bring it indoors, it will carry with it the fragrance of fresh air and flowers.

"Such is the case with the mind. Your garment of thoughts absorbs the vibrations of those with whom you mix. If you mingle with pessimists, in time you will become a pessimist. And if you mingle with cheerful, happy people, you yourself will develop a cheerful, happy nature.

"Environment is stronger than will power. To mix with worldly people without absorbing at least some of their worldliness requires great spiritual strength.

"Beginners on the spiritual path, especially, should be very careful in the company they keep. They should mix with other devotees, and try not to mingle with ego-saturated, worldly people. They should especially avoid people who are negative, even if those people are devotees.

"Whether one becomes a saint or a sinner is to a great extent determined by the company he keeps."

⤙13⤚

"It is better to live in hell with one wise man than in heaven with ten fools."

⤙14⤚

"Churned milk turns to butter, which floats on water. Whole milk, however, mingles with water and is diluted by it.

"Even so, once the mind has been 'churned' to the 'butter' of Self-realization it is no longer affected by worldly influences. The ordinary devotee, however, must choose his company carefully. If possible, he should strictly avoid environments that are incompatible with his inner search for God."

⤙15⤚

"Life will bring you many ups and downs. If you let your feelings rise and fall with the waves of circumstance, you will never attain that inner calmness which is the foundation of spiritual progress. Be careful, therefore, not to react emotionally. Rise above likes and dislikes.

"A good rule to live by, and one that will take you sailing through many tests in life, is, under all circumstances, to remain *even-minded and cheerful.*"

16

"Whenever you see wrong in others, and are distressed by it, remember, it's wrong with you. When you are right inwardly, all things are right, for you see everything as part of God. You then accept all things as they are, without judgment, and look with kindness and sympathy on everyone, no matter how foolish."

17

A certain disciple was inclined to be moody. "If you want to be sad," the Master told her, "no one in the world can make you happy. But if you make up your mind to be happy, no one and nothing on earth can take that happiness from you."

18

"You can't love God and at the same time be unkind to your associates. You can't love Him and be full of wrath. How you behave toward others both reflects your inner consciousness and conditions it."

~19~

"Never imagine that you can win God's love if you can't win the love of your fellow creatures. As you love Him, so should you love Him in all."

~20~

"Don't judge your inner progress by what others think of you, unless you know their discrimination to be dependable. For people usually praise or criticize others for all the wrong reasons. They like a thing if it endorses their opinions, however mistaken; and they dislike anything if it poses a threat to those opinions.

"Accept both praise and criticism with equanimity.

"If, however, you must prefer one of these to the other, then prefer criticism.

"There was a saint in India whose evening gatherings with the disciples were often disturbed by a skeptical neighbor, who made it a point to find fault with everything the saint said or did. The disciples kept wanting to throw him out, but the Master wouldn't hear of it.

"One evening a disciple appeared at the evening discussion sporting a broad smile. 'Master,' he cried exultantly, 'your enemy, the critic, is dead!'

"'Ah, alas!' cried the saint, tears welling up in his eyes. 'I am heartbroken. My best friend has left this world. He was the only one who was willing to help me by pointing out my faults. Shall I ever find another as true to my well-being as he?'"

⇢⇥ 21 ⇠⇤

To a disciple who was bowed by the weight of spiritual doubts, Yogananda said, "Don't depend on reason. That is where Satan tricks you. Reason is like a sword with a smooth handle. If you haven't mastered its use, it can prove dangerous. One clumsy move, and instead of striking the enemy you may injure yourself.

"The moment doubt enters your mind, cast it out. Drown it in activity for God. Recognize it as a temptation from Satan.

"Krishna said in the Bhagavad Gita, 'The doubter, O Arjuna, is the most miserable of mortals.'"

⇢⇥ 22 ⇠⇤

"There are two kinds of doubt: destructive and constructive.

"Destructive doubt is habitual skepticism. People who cultivate this attitude are as blind in their disbelief as any bigot in his bigotry. For such people, impartial investigation has no relevance. They want only that information which will negate new ideas, and which agrees with their own, or with the prevailing, opinions.

"Skepticism is like static in the radio of the mind. It prevents a person from receiving the broadcasts of intuition from the silence within.

"Constructive doubt, on the other hand, is intelligent questioning, and fair, impartial examination. Those who cultivate this attitude never prejudge an idea. Nor do they accept as valid the unsubstantiated opinions of others. They keep an open mind, and base their conclusions on objective tests. They seek above all to verify those conclusions by their own experience.

"This is the proper approach to truth."

⇢ 23 ⇠

A disciple was plagued by self-doubt. Yogananda tried often to encourage him, but with limited success. One day he told the disciple:

"Thoughts have materializing power. Beware lest, through fear, you attract the very circumstances which you dread. God is blessing you constantly, but by your doubts you close yourself to His grace, which would dispel your delusions.

"Swami Shankara," he continued, "had a woman student who used to come to him all the time with fears and doubts. 'What if this should happen?' she would moan, or, 'What if I should do that?'

"One day this woman said to him, 'But—supposing I die?'

"Shankara looked at her calmly and said, 'All right, then, die!' And the woman fell lifeless to the ground.

"It wasn't that Swami Shankara was responsible for her death. He simply allowed her own thought-force to materialize at last, as it would have done much sooner without his blessings. Thus, her soul received a severe lesson, which the guru had been trying in vain to help her to learn by gentler means."

⟶ 24 ⟵

"Your mental attitudes are important. Spiritual progress isn't only a matter of practicing the yoga techniques!

"Every time you think good thoughts, the *kundalini*[2] begins to move upward. Every time you hate people or hold harsh thoughts about them, the *kundalini* automatically moves downward. When you love others selflessly, or think kind thoughts about them, it moves up the spine.

"*Kundalini* is not awakened by techniques alone."

⟶ 25 ⟵

"Always affirm inwardly, 'I am ageless. I am eternal. I live in timelessness. I was created before the galaxies were formed.'"

-»≡26≡«-

"No matter how far away God seems from you, live always in the thought that you belong with Him.

"And no matter how real your material life appears, and how real your attachment to it seems, hold it at a distance by reminding yourself of its impermanence.

"A blade of grass looks tiny when you hold it at arm's length, but when you bring it up close to your eye it appears large. Even so, the experiences of this life seem important to you ('as big as life'—isn't that the expression?) only because you hold them so close to you. You allow them completely to possess your thoughts and feelings.

"Distance yourself from them mentally, even a little bit, and you will quickly realize their insignificance relative to the vast truth that beckons to you from Infinity."

---

1 See footnote, p. 106
2 The life-force, as it flows down the spine from the brain during the creation of the physical body, becomes polarized. The positive pole is centered in the frontal lobe of the brain at a point midway between the eyebrows. The negative pole is centered at the base of the spine in the coccyx region.

The energy at this negative pole represents the "end of the line," so to speak, for the outward movement of the life-force in its impulse to enter the material world. Negative energy thus becomes locked there. It must be wooed from its outward commitment, and directed back toward the brain, for spiritual enlightenment to occur. This focal point of negative energy is called *kundalini*. Hence, much attention is given in the yoga teachings to the awakening of *kundalini*.

St. Teresa of Avila described the experience of this force—without, of course, giving it a name. "In ecstasy," she wrote, "the soul flies upward like a bullet being shot out of a gun." —*ed.*

Chapter 20

SELF-REALIZATION

⊶ 1 ⊷

"Once the mind is interiorized," Paramhansa Yogananda said, "and withdrawn from its identification with the world and with the body, the inner light comes into clear and steady focus. The inner sounds become all-absorbing. *Aum* fills the brain; its vibration moves down the spine, bursting open the door of the heart's feeling, then flowing out into the body. The whole body vibrates with the sound of *Aum.*

"Gradually, with ever-deeper meditation, the consciousness expands with that sound. Moving beyond the confines of the body, it embraces the vastness of infinite vibration. You realize your oneness with all existence as *Aum*, the Cosmic Vibration.

"This state is known as *Aum samadhi*, or union with God as Cosmic Sound. *Aum* is that aspect of the Christian Trinity which is known as the Holy Ghost, or Word of God.

"By still deeper meditation, one perceives in the physical body, underlying the *Aum* vibration, the vibrationless calm of the Christ consciousness, the reflection in creation of the unmoving Spirit beyond creation.

"In ancient spiritual tradition, the Christ consciousness is spoken of as the Son. For just as, among human beings, the son is a reflection of the father, so in Cosmic consciousness the Christ—in Sanskrit called Krishna, or *Kutastha Chaitanya*—reflects in all things the consciousness of God, the Father, beyond creation.

"By ever deeper meditation, one expands his awareness of the Christ consciousness beyond the limits of the body to perceive his oneness finally with the Christ consciousness, which underlies the manifested universe.

"By deeper meditation still, one goes beyond creation and unites his consciousness with that of the Father, *Satchidananda*, the vast ocean of Spirit.

"In these progressive stages of realization are discovered, in reverse order, the three aspects of the Trinity: Father, Son, and Holy Ghost.

"Jesus was called the Christ. Most people are not aware that Christ wasn't the name given him at birth. It was a title signifying 'the anointed of God,' or, 'chosen by God.'[1]

"In the same way, Krishna in India was really Jadava *the* Krishna—or *Christna*, as it is sometimes written to show that the meaning is the same.

"Jesus was a master. He had attained Christ consciousness. Anyone who attains that state of consciousness may justifiably also be called the Christ, for he has dissolved his ego in the infinite consciousness.

"*Aum*, the Holy Ghost, is also referred to in ancient traditions as the Mother, for it represents the feminine aspect of God.

"The Roman Catholic Church teaches that one must go through the Mother to reach Christ. To them, of course, the Mother signifies Mary, the mother of Jesus. For all that, the truth is there, though far deeper than the generally accepted understanding of it.

"For, to reach Christ consciousness, you must first unite your consciousness with *Aum*, the Cosmic Vibration.

"Self-realization means the realization that your true Self is not the ego, but God, the vast ocean of Spirit which manifested for a time the little wave of awareness that you now see as yourself."

‑⇒ 2 ⇐‑

"I've read that the Christian Trinity is the same as the Hindu Trinity of Brahma, Vishnu, and Shiva," remarked a student of comparative religions. "Is this true?"

"No," replied Paramhansa Yogananda. "Brahma, Vishnu, and Shiva personify the three aspects of *Aum*, the vibration that creates, preserves, and destroys the universe. Hence, Brahma the Creator, Vishnu the Preserver, and Shiva the Destroyer.

"*Aum*, which is often written OM in English, with two letters, is more correctly rendered with three letters, *AUM*. The first letter, *A*, represents the creative vibration; the second, *U*, represents the preserving vibration; and the third letter, *M*, represents the vibration of destruction—that which dissolves the created universe back into the Infinite Silence.

"In English, *Aum* is often written with two letters as OM, because the English *O* is a diphthong, and because most people, when reading *Aum*, pronounce the *A* long as in 'car.' This long *A* is an error. 'OM' is the correct pronunciation.

"*Aum* is traditionally chanted three times, as a reminder of its three aspects. The first time, it is sung high; the second, lower; and the third, lower still. These are the differences in sound between the three vibrations of the cosmic sound. Brahma, the creative vibration, is high-pitched; Vishnu, the preservative vibration, is pitched somewhat lower; and Shiva, the all-dissolving vibration, is a low, deep sound.

"The Hindu Trinity that is equivalent to the Trinity of Christianity is called *Aum-Tat-Sat: Aum*, the Holy Ghost; *Tat*, the *Kutastha Chaitanya*, or Christ consciousness; and *Sat*, the Father aspect of God, the Spirit beyond all vibration. *Sat* means 'existence.' It was further defined by Swami Shankaracharya as *satchidananda*, which I have translated as 'ever-existing, ever-conscious, ever-new bliss.'"[2]

→⇒ 3 ⇐←

A disciple inquired, "When may someone be called a master?"

"One is a master," Paramhansa Yogananda replied, "when he has attained Christ consciousness."

→⇒ 4 ⇐←

"Your teachings clarify marvelously the writings of the great Christian mystics," exclaimed a student of those writings.

"The truth is ever simple," replied the Master, "even though, in its very simplicity, it is not often easy for the human mind to assimilate. The bird that is born in a cage cannot easily believe that its true nature is to soar freely over brooks and meadows. Even so, the human mind finds it difficult to imagine its native freedom in omnipresence.

"It is a misnomer, however, to call those great souls, 'mystics.' Divine truth is not mystical! People think of the material world as the reality, and of that inner realm as vague and indistinct. They are mistaken. The real mystery is why so many people remain content with this illusory world, and devote so little energy to seeking the Truth behind it.

"The real vagueness lies in people's own perception of truth. Worldly people then, not the saints, are the real 'mystics'!

"Mysticism is a misnomer also because it encourages vagueness in people's spiritual endeavors. It becomes easy, once the mind accepts vagueness as an acceptable approach to truth, to wander about in the misty world of subconscious imagination instead of exerting the will power and concentration necessary to enter superconsciousness."

-⤖5⬻-

"What is *samadhi*?" asked a visitor. "I've read about it in books, but I'm afraid it has no clear meaning for me."

"*Samadhi*," Yogananda replied, "is the realization that you are much more than this physical body. By 'realization' I don't mean an intellectual grasp. 'Realizations' of that sort are imaginary. I mean the state of being in which one is actually conscious of himself in all space, everywhere.

"I remarked to someone the other day, 'You have a sour taste in your mouth, haven't you?'

"'How did you know?' he inquired. He was very astonished.

"'I know,' I replied, 'because I am just as much in your body as I am in this one.'

"In *samadhi* you know what is going on at a distance. Indeed, for you it is not distant. Your consciousness embraces omnipresence. You see the human body as an infinitesimal part of your infinite reality.

"There are two stages of *samadhi*. In the first, the consciousness merges into the Infinite during meditation. The yogi cannot preserve that state, however, once he comes out of his meditation. That state is known as *sabikalpa samadhi*.

"The next state is called *nirbikalpa samadhi*. In this state of consciousness you maintain your divine realization even while working or speaking or moving about in this world. *Nirbikalpa* is the highest realization. Once attaining that, there is no further possibility of falling back into delusion.

"I made this distinction in a chant I once wrote:
"'In *sabikalpa samadhi* yoga
I will drown myself in my Self.
In *nirbikalpa samadhi* yoga
I will find myself in my Self.'

"Jesus Christ also spoke of drowning the little self in the infinite Self. He said, 'For whosoever will save his life shall lose it: and whosoever will lose his life for my sake shall find it.'"[3]

— 6 —

"There was a devotee who was sitting before an image of his guru, chanting and tossing flowers onto it as an expression of his devotion. His concentration became so deep that, all at once, he beheld the whole universe contained within his consciousness.

"'Ah!' he cried, 'I have been putting flowers on another's image, but now I see that I, untouched by this body, am the Sustainer of the universe. I bow to my Self!' And he began throwing the flowers onto his own head."

— 7 —

"Self-realization is the knowing in all parts of body, mind, and soul that you are now in possession of the kingdom of God; that you do not have to pray that it come to you; that God's omnipresence is your omnipresence; and that all that you need to do is improve your knowing."

--⊷8⊶--

"When will you find God? When all your desires for other things are finished. When you realize that the only thing worth having is Him. When every thought, every feeling is drenched with the love of God."

1   Luke 23:35.
2   The names, Bramha, Vishnu, and Shiva, each taken by itself rather than as part of a trinity, are used individually also in reference to the Absolute Spirit.—*ed.*
3   Matthew 16:25.

INDEX

The references in this index are by chapter and quotation number. Page numbers are also listed, in parentheses. Thus, for example, the citation 5:2,7-(30) refers to chapter five, quotations number two and seven; quotation two begins on page 30.

ABOUT THE AUTHOR

"As a bright light shining in the midst of darkness, so was Yogananda's presence in this world. Such a great soul comes on earth only rarely, when there is a real need among men."
—The Shankaracharya of Kanchipuram

PARAMHANSA YOGANANDA

Born in India in 1893, Paramhansa Yogananda was trained from his early years to bring India's ancient science of Self-realization to the West. In 1920 he moved to the United States to begin what was to develop into a worldwide work touching millions of lives. Americans were hungry for India's spiritual teachings, and for the liberating techniques of yoga.

In 1946 he published what has become a spiritual classic and one of the best-loved books of the 20th century, *Autobiography of a Yogi*. In addition, Yogananda established the headquarters for a worldwide work, wrote a number of books and study courses, gave lectures to many thousands in most major cities across the United States, wrote music and poetry, and trained disciples. He was invited to the White House by Calvin Coolidge, and he initiated Mahatma Gandhi into Kriya Yoga, his most advanced technique of meditation.

Yogananda's message to the West highlighted the unity of all religions, and the importance of love for God combined with scientific techniques of meditation.

About the Editor

"Swami Kriyananda is a man of wisdom and compassion in action, truly one of the leading lights in the spiritual world today."
—Lama Surya Das, Dzogchen Center, author *of Awakening The Buddha Within*

Swami Kriyananda

A prolific author, accomplished composer, playwright, and artist, and a world-renowned spiritual teacher, Swami Kriyananda refers to himself simply as "a humble disciple" of the great God-realized master, Paramhansa Yogananda. He met his guru at the young age of twenty-two, and served him during the last four years of the Master's life. And he has done so continuously ever since.

Kriyananda was born in Rumania of American parents, and educated in Europe, England, and the United States. Philosophically and artistically inclined from youth, he soon came to question life's meaning and society's values. During a period of intense inward reflection, he discovered Yogananda's *Autobiography of a Yogi*, and immediately traveled 3,000 miles from New York to California to meet the Master, who accepted him as a monastic disciple. Yogananda appointed him as the head of the monastery, authorized him to teach in his name and to give initiation into Kriya Yoga, and entrusted him with the missions of writing and developing what he called "world-brotherhood colonies."

Recognized as the "father of the spiritual communities movement" in the United States, Swami Kriyananda founded the Ananda World Brotherhood Community in the Sierra Nevada Foothills of Northern California in 1968. It has served as a model for seven communities founded subsequently in the United States, Europe, and India.

In 2003 Swami Kriyananda, then in his seventy-eighth year, moved to India with a small international group of disciples, to dedicate his remaining years to making his guru's teachings better known. He appears daily on Indian national television with his program *A Way of Awakening*. He has established Ananda Sangha Publications, which publishes many of his 90 literary works and spreads the teachings of Kriya Yoga throughout India. His vision for the next years includes founding cooperative spiritual communities in India (there are two communites now in India, one in Gurgaon and the other in Pune); a temple of all religions dedicated to Paramhansa Yogananda; a retreat center; a school system; a monastery; as well as a university-level Yoga Institute of Living Wisdom.

MORE YOGANANDA TITLES

The original 1946 unedited edition of
Yogananda's spiritual masterpiece

AUTOBIOGRAPHY OF A YOGI
by Paramhansa Yogananda

Autobiography of a Yogi is one of the best-selling
Eastern philosophy titles of all time, with
millions of copies sold, named one of the best and
most influential books of the twentieth century.
This highly prized reprinting of the original
1946 edition is the only one available free from
textual changes made after Yogananda's death.
Yogananda was the first yoga master of India
whose mission was to live and teach in the West.

In this updated edition are bonus materials, including a last chapter that
Yogananda wrote in 1951, without posthumous changes. This new edition
also includes the eulogy that Yogananda wrote for Gandhi, and a new
foreword and afterword by Swami Kriyananda, one of Yogananda's close,
direct disciples.

This edition of *Autobiography of a Yogi* is also available in unabridged
audiobook (MP3) format, read by Swami Kriyananda, Yogananda's direct
disciple.

Praise for Autobiography of a Yogi

*"In the original edition, published during Yogananda's life, one is more in
contact with Yogananda himself. While Yogananda founded centers and
organizations, his concern was more with guiding individuals to direct communion with Divinity rather than with promoting any one church as opposed
to another. This spirit is easier to grasp in the original edition of this great
spiritual and yogic classic."*

— David Frawley, Director, American Institute of Vedic Studies,
author of *Yoga and Ayurveda*

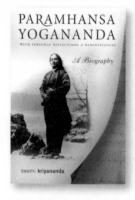

PARAMHANSA YOGANANDA
A Biography with Personal Reflections and Reminiscences
by Swami Kriyananda

Paramhansa Yogananda's classic *Autobiography of a Yogi* is more about the saints Yogananda met than about himself—in spite of the fact that Yogananda was much greater than many he described. Now, one of Yogananda's few remaining direct disciples relates the untold story of this great spiritual master and world teacher: his teenage miracles, his challenges in coming to America, his national lecture campaigns, his struggles to fulfill his world-changing mission amid incomprehension and painful betrayals, and his ultimate triumphant achievement. Kriyananda's subtle grasp of his guru's inner nature reveals Yogananda's many-sided greatness. Includes many never-before-published anecdotes.

THE NEW PATH
My Life with Paramhansa Yogananda
by Swami Kriyananda

This is the moving story of Kriyananda's years with Paramhansa Yogananda, India's emissary to the West and the first yoga master to spend the greater part of his life in America. When Swami Kriyananda discovered *Autobiography of a Yogi* in 1948, he was totally new to Eastern teachings. This is a great advantage to the Western reader, since Kriyananda walks us along the yogic path as he discovers it from the moment of his initiation as a disciple of Yogananda. With winning honesty, humor, and deep insight, he shares his journey on the spiritual path through personal stories and experiences. Through more than four hundred stories of life with Yogananda, we tune in more deeply to this great master and to the teachings he brought to the West. This book is an ideal complement to *Autobiography of a Yogi*.

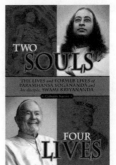

TWO SOULS: FOUR LIVES
The Lives and Former Lives of Paramhansa
Yogananda and his disciple, Swami Kriyananda
Catherine Kairavi

This book explores an astonishing statement
made by Paramhansa Yogananda, that he was the
historical figure, William the Conqueror, in a
previous incarnation.

The Norman Conquest of England was one of the
pivotal moments in world history, a series of events that affects us even
today. Is it possible that two of the greatest men of that era—William the
Conqueror and his son, Henry I of England—have recently reincarnated
as the great spiritual master Paramhansa Yogananda (author of the classic
Autobiography of a Yogi) and his close disciple, Swami Kriyananda? If so,
what are the subtle connections between the Norman Conquest and
modern times?

THE ESSENCE OF THE BHAGAVAD GITA
Explained by Paramhansa Yogananda
As Remembered by his disciple, Swami Kriyananda

Rarely in a lifetime does a new spiritual classic
appear that has the power to change people's lives
and transform future generations. This is such a
book. This revelation of India's best-loved scripture
approaches it from a fresh perspective, showing its
deep allegorical meaning and its down-to-earth
practicality. The themes presented are universal:
how to achieve victory in life in union with the divine; how to prepare for
life's "final exam," death, and what happens afterward; how to triumph over
all pain and suffering.

"A brilliant text that will greatly enhance the spiritual life of every reader."
—Caroline Myss, author of *Anatomy of the Spirit and Sacred Contracts*

*"It is doubtful that there has been a more important spiritual writing in
the last fifty years than this soul-stirring, monumental work. What a gift!
What a treasure!"*
—Neale Donald Walsch, author of *Conversations with God*

REVELATIONS OF CHRIST
Proclaimed by Paramhansa Yogananda
Presented by his disciple, Swami Kriyananda

The rising tide of alternative beliefs proves that now, more than ever, people are yearning for a clear-minded and uplifting understanding of the life and teachings of Jesus Christ. This galvanizing book, presenting the teachings of Christ from the experience and perspective of Paramhansa Yogananda, one of the greatest spiritual masters of the twentieth century, finally offers the fresh perspective on Christ's teachings for which the world has been waiting. *Revelations of Christ* presents us with an opportunity to understand and apply the scriptures in a more reliable way than any other: by studying under those saints who have communed directly, in deep ecstasy, with Christ and God.

"This is a great gift to humanity. It is a spiritual treasure to cherish and to pass on to children for generations."

—Neale Donald Walsch, author of *Conversations with God*

"Kriyananda's revelatory book gives us the enlightened, timeless wisdom of Jesus the Christ in a way that addresses the challenges of twenty-first century living."

—Michael Beckwith, Founder and Spiritual Director,
Agape International Spiritual Center, author of *Inspirations of the Heart*

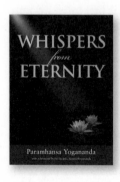

WHISPERS FROM ETERNITY
Paramhansa Yogananda
Edited by his disciple, Swami Kriyananda

Many poetic works can inspire, but few, like this one, have the power to change your life. Yogananda was not only a spiritual master, but a master poet, whose verses revealed the hidden divine presence behind even everyday things. This book has the power to rapidly accelerate your spiritual growth, and provides hundreds of delightful ways for you to begin your own conversation with God.

Swami Kriyananda (J. Donald Walters)

CONVERSATIONS WITH YOGANANDA
Recorded, Compiled, and Edited with commentary by his disciple Swami Kriyananda

This is an unparalleled, first-hand account of the teachings of Paramhansa Yogananda. Featuring nearly 500 never-before-released stories, sayings, and insights, this is an extensive, yet eminently accessible treasure trove of wisdom from one of the 20th Century's most famous yoga masters.

"A wonderful book! To find a previously unknown message from Yogananda now is an extraordinary spiritual gift. Open up at random for an encouraging word from one of the century's most beloved spiritual teachers."
—**Neale Donald Walsch**, author of *Conversations with God*

~ The WISDOM of YOGANANDA series ~

Six volumes of Paramhansa Yogananda's timeless wisdom in an approachable, easy-to-read format. The writings of the Master are presented with minimal editing, to capture his expansive and compassionate wisdom, his sense of fun, and his practical spiritual guidance.

HOW TO BE HAPPY ALL THE TIME
The Wisdom of Yogananda Series, VOLUME 1

Yogananda powerfully explains virtually everything needed to lead a happier, more fulfilling life. Topics include: looking for happiness in the right places; choosing to be happy; tools and techniques for achieving happiness; sharing happiness with others; balancing success and happiness; and many more.

KARMA & REINCARNATION
The Wisdom of Yogananda Series, VOLUME 2

Yogananda reveals the truth behind karma, death, reincarnation, and the afterlife. With clarity and simplicity, he makes the mysterious understandable. Topics include: why we see a world of suffering and inequality; how to handle the challenges in our lives; what happens at death, and after death; and the purpose of reincarnation.

SPIRITUAL RELATIONSHIPS
The Wisdom of Yogananda Series, VOLUME 3

This book contains practical guidance and fresh insight on relationships of all types. Topics include: how to cure bad habits that can end true friendship; how to choose the right partner; sex in marriage and how to conceive a spiritual child; problems that arise in marriage; the Universal Love behind all your relationships.

HOW TO BE A SUCCESS
The Wisdom of Yogananda Series, VOLUME 4

This book includes the complete text of The Attributes of Success, the original booklet later published as The Law of Success. In addition, you will learn how to find your purpose in life, develop habits of success and eradicate habits of failure, develop your will power and magnetism, and thrive in the right job.

HOW TO HAVE COURAGE, CALMNESS, & CONFIDENCE
The Wisdom of Yogananda Series, VOLUME 5

~ Winner of the 2011 International Book Award for Best Self-Help Title ~

This book shows you how to transform your life. Dislodge negative thoughts and depression. Uproot fear and thoughts of failure. Cure nervousness and systematically eliminate worry from your life. Overcome anger, sorrow, over-sensitivity, and a host of other troublesome emotional responses; and much more.

HOW TO ACHIEVE GLOWING HEALTH & VITALITY
The Wisdom of Yogananda Series, volume 6

Paramhansa Yogananda, a foremost spiritual teacher of modern times, offers practical, wide-ranging, and fascinating suggestions on how to have more energy and live a radiantly healthy life. The principles in this book promote physical health and all-round well-being, mental clarity, and ease and inspiration in your spiritual life. Readers will discover the priceless Energization Exercises for rejuvenating the body and mind, the fine art of conscious relaxation, and helpful diet tips for health and beauty.

FURTHER EXPLORATIONS

THE RUBAIYAT OF OMAR KHAYYAM EXPLAINED
Paramhansa Yogananda,
edited by Swami Kriyananda

The Rubaiyat is loved by Westerners as a hymn of praise to sensual delights. In the East its quatrains are considered a deep allegory of the soul's romance with God, based solely on the author Omar Khayyam's reputation as a sage and mystic. But for centuries the meaning of this famous poem has remained a mystery. Now Yogananda reveals the secret meaning and the golden spiritual treasures hidden behind the Rubaiyat's verses, and presents a new scripture to the world.

THE BHAGAVAD GITA
According to Paramhansa Yogananda
Edited by Swami Kriyananda

This translation of the Gita, by Paramhansa Yogananda, brings alive the deep spiritual insights and poetic beauty of the famous battlefield dialogue between Krishna and Arjuna. Based on the little-known truth that each character in the Gita represents an aspect of our own being, it expresses with revelatory clarity how to win the struggle within between the forces of our lower and higher natures.

GOD IS FOR EVERYONE
Inspired by Paramhansa Yogananda
by Swami Kriyananda

This book presents a concept of God and spiritual meaning that will broadly appeal to everyone, from the most uncertain agnostic to the most fervent believer. Clearly and simply written, thoroughly non-sectarian and non-dogmatic in its approach, it is the perfect introduction to the spiritual path. Yogananda's core teachings are presented by his disciple, Swami Kriyananda.

AWAKEN TO SUPERCONSCIOUSNESS
by Swami Kriyananda

This popular guide includes everything you need to know about the philosophy and practice of meditation, and how to apply the meditative mind to resolve common daily conflicts in uncommon, superconscious ways. Superconsciousness is the hidden mechanism at work behind intuition, spiritual and physical healing, successful problem solving, and finding deep and lasting joy.

THE ART & SCIENCE OF RAJA YOGA
by Swami Kriyananda

Contains fourteen lessons in which the original yoga science emerges in all its glory—a proven system for realizing one's spiritual destiny. This is the most comprehensive course available on yoga and meditation today. Over 450 pages of text and photos give you a complete and detailed presentation of yoga postures, yoga philosophy, affirmations, meditation instruction, and breathing techniques. Also included are suggestions for daily yoga routines, information on proper diet, recipes, and alternative healing techniques. The book also comes with an audio CD that contains: a guided yoga postures sessions, a guided meditation, and an inspiring talk on how you can use these techniques to solve many of the problems of daily life.

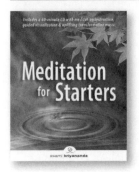

MEDITATION FOR STARTERS
by Swami Kriyananda

If you have wanted to learn to meditate, but never had a chance, this is the place to start. Filled with easy-to-follow instructions, beautiful guided visualizations, and answers to important questions on meditation, the book includes: what meditation is (and isn't); how to relax your body and prepare yourself for going within; and techniques for interiorizing and focusing the mind. Includes a 60-minute companion CD with guided visualization and meditation instruction.

RELIGION IN THE NEW AGE
Swami Kriyananda

Our planet has entered an "Age of Energy" that will affect us for centuries to come. We can see evidence of this all around us: in ultra-fast computers, the quickening of communication and transportation, and the shrinking of time and space. This fascinating book of essays explores how this new age will change our lives, especially our spiritual seeking. Covers a wide range of upcoming societal shifts — in leadership, relationships, and self-development — including the movement away from organized religion to inner experience.

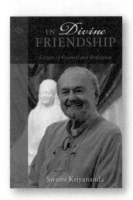

IN DIVINE FRIENDSHIP
Swami Kriyananda

This extraordinary book of nearly 250 letters, written over a thirty-year period by Swami Kriyananda, responds to practically any concern a spiritual seeker might have, such as: strengthening one's faith, accelerating one's spiritual progress, meditating more deeply, responding to illness, earning a living, attracting a mate, raising children, overcoming negative self-judgments, and responding to world upheavals.

Connecting all of these letters is the love, compassion, and wisdom of Swami Kriyananda, one of the leading spiritual figures of our time. The letters describe in detail his efforts to fulfill his Guru's commission to establish spiritual communities, and offer invaluable advice to leaders everywhere on how to avoid the temptations of materialism, selfishness, and pride. A spiritual treasure that speaks to truth seekers at all levels.

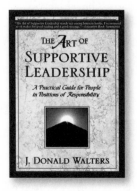

THE ART OF SUPPORTIVE LEADERSHIP
A Practical Guide for People in Positions of Responsibility
J. Donald Walters (Swami Kriyananda)

You can learn to be a more effective leader by viewing leadership in terms of shared accomplishments rather than personal advancement. Drawn from timeless Eastern wisdom, this book is clear, concise, and practical—designed from the start to produce results quickly and simply.

Used in training seminars in the U.S., Europe, and India, this book gives practical advice for leaders and potential leaders to help increase effectiveness, creativity, and team building. Individual entrepreneurs, corporations such as Kellogg, military and police personnel, and non-profit organizations are using this approach.

MONEY MAGNETISM
How to Attract What You Need When You Need It
J. Donald Walters (Swami Kriyananda)

This book can change your life by transforming how you think and feel about money. According to the author, anyone can attract wealth: "There need be no limits to the flow of your abundance." Through numerous true stories and examples, Swami Kriyananda vividly—sometimes humorously—shows you how and why the principles of money magnetism work, and how you can immediately start applying them to achieve greater success in your material and your spiritual life.

METAPHYSICAL MEDITATIONS
Swami Kriyananda

Kriyananda's soothing voice guides you in thirteen different meditations based on the soul-inspiring, mystical poetry of Paramhansa Yogananda. Each meditation is accompanied by beautiful classical music to help you quiet your thoughts and prepare for deep states of meditation. Includes a full recitation of Yogananda's poem "Samadhi," which appears in *Autobiography of a Yogi*. A great aid to the serious meditator, as well as to those just beginning their practice.

MEDITATIONS TO AWAKEN SUPERCONSCIOUSNESS
Guided Meditations on the Light
Swami Kriyananda

Featuring two beautiful guided meditations as well as an introductory section to help prepare the listener for meditation, this extraordinary recording of visualizations can be used either by itself, or as a companion to the book, *Awaken to Superconsciousness*. The soothing, transformative words, spoken over inspiring sitar background music, creates one of the most unique guided meditation products available.

RELAX: MEDITATIONS FOR FLUTE AND CELLO
Donald Walters
Featuring David Eby and Sharon Nani

This CD is specifically designed to slow respiration and heart rate, bringing listeners to their calm center. This recording features fifteen melodies for flute and cello, accompanied by harp, guitar, keyboard, and strings. Excellent for creating a calming atmosphere for work and home.

AUM: MANTRA OF ETERNITY
Swami Kriyananda

This recording features nearly seventy minutes of continuous vocal chanting of AUM, the Sanskrit word meaning peace and oneness of spirit. AUM, the cosmic creative vibration, is extensively discussed by Yogananda in *Autobiography of a Yogi*. Chanted here by his disciple, Kriyananda, this recording is a stirring way to tune into this cosmic power.

Other titles in the Mantra Series:

Gayatri Mantra*
Mahamrityanjaya Mantra*
Maha Mantra*

BLISS CHANTS
Ananda Kirtan

Chanting focuses and lifts the mind to higher states of consciousness. *Bliss Chants* features chants written by Yogananda and his direct disciple, Swami Kriyananda. They're performed by Ananda Kirtan, a group of singers and musicians from Ananda, one of the world's most respected yoga communities. Chanting is accompanied by guitar, harmonium, kirtals, and tabla.

Other titles in the Chant Series:

Divine Mother Chants   Power Chants
Love Chants   Peace Chants
Wisdom Chants*   Wellness Chants*

Visit our website to view all our available titles in books, audiobooks, spoken word, music and DVDs.

www.crystalclarity.com

* Coming Soon

CRYSTAL CLARITY PUBLISHERS

Crystal Clarity Publishers offers additional resources to assist you in your spiritual journey including many other books, a wide variety of inspirational and relaxation music composed by Swami Kriyananda, and yoga and meditation videos. To see a complete listing of our products, contact us for a print catalog or see our website: www.crystalclarity.com

Crystal Clarity Publishers

14618 Tyler Foote Rd., Nevada City, CA 95959

TOLL FREE: 800.424.1055 or 530.478.7600 / FAX: 530.478.7610

EMAIL: clarity@crystalclarity.com

ANANDA WORLDWIDE

Ananda Sangha, a worldwide organization founded by Swami Kriyananda, offers spiritual support and resources based on the teachings of Paramhansa Yogananda. There are Ananda spiritual communities in Nevada City, Sacramento, and Palo Alto, California; Seattle, Washington; Portland, Oregon; as well as a retreat center and European community in Assisi, Italy, and communities near New Delhi and Pune, India. Ananda supports more than 75 meditation groups worldwide.

For more information about Ananda Sangha communities or meditation groups near you, please call 530.478.7560 or visit www.ananda.org.

THE EXPANDING LIGHT

Ananda's guest retreat, The Expanding Light, offers a varied, year-round schedule of classes and workshops on yoga, meditation, and spiritual practice. You may also come for a relaxed personal renewal, participating in ongoing activities as much or as little as you wish. The beautiful serene mountain setting, supportive staff, and delicious vegetarian food provide an ideal environment for a truly meaningful, spiritual vacation.

For more information, please call 800.346.5350

or visit www.expandinglight.org.